What people are

FRANCHISING
McCHURCH

"What's wrong with multisite churches? Thomas White and John Mark Yeats have written a book that tells us. This book tackles current, thorny issues with both criticism and grace—inflated membership statistics, plagiarizing sermons, multiple services, and video pastors. White and Yeats say that consumerism is killing churches. This is the best, most thorough treatment of these topics that I've read. In fact, it's the book many of us have been waiting for. I couldn't put it down."

Mark Dever, senior pastor of Capitol Hill Baptist Church, Washington, DC, and director of 9Marks.org

"In *Franchising McChurch*, John Mark Yeats and Thomas White have penned a clever and biblically compelling book that may ruffle feathers and cut against the grain. They explain more than some people will want to contemplate the appalling state of biblical illiteracy and therefore moral fiber that has become characteristic of church life in America in the early years of the twenty-first century. Only the courageous should venture into the pages of this book. No wimps allowed!"

Paige Patterson, president of Southwestern Baptist Theological Seminary, Fort Worth, Texas

"Many thanks to White and Yeats for this prophetic and timely book. I pray that God will use it to renew our faith in the ministry of His Word and Holy Spirit. We have indeed grown fat and lazy, too dependent for our spiritual lives on famous people, marketing, and flashy entertainment. We need God's own nutrition, 'solid food' fit for 'the mature' (Heb. 5:11–14). Lord, have mercy on our culture, on our evangelical culture. Encourage us, we pray, to get off the couch and follow You."

Douglas A. Sweeney, Trinity Evangelical Divinity School

FRANCHISING McCHURCH

FEEDING OUR OBSESSION WITH EASY CHRISTIANITY

THOMAS WHITE & JOHN M. YEATS

David C Cook®

transforming lives together

FRANCHISING McCHURCH
Published by David C. Cook
4050 Lee Vance View
Colorado Springs, CO 80918 U.S.A.

David C. Cook Distribution Canada
55 Woodslee Avenue, Paris, Ontario, Canada N3L 3E5

David C. Cook U.K., Kingsway Communications
Eastbourne, East Sussex BN23 6NT, England

David C. Cook and the graphic circle C logo
are registered trademarks of Cook Communications Ministries.

The Web site addresses recommended throughout this book are offered as a resource to you. These Web sites are not intended in any way to be or imply an endorsement on the part of David C. Cook, nor do we vouch for their content.

All Scripture quotations, unless otherwise noted, are taken from the *New American Standard Bible*, © Copyright 1960, 1995 by The Lockman Foundation. Used by permission. Scripture quotations marked NKJV are taken from the New King James Version. Copyright © 1982 by Thomas Nelson, Inc. Used by permission. All rights reserved. Italics in Scripture are added by the authors for emphasis.

LCCN 2008941138
ISBN 978-1-4347-0004-9

© 2009 Thomas White and John M. Yeats

The Team: John Blase, Michael Klassen, Amy Kiechlin, Jaci Schneider,
Karen Athen, and Susan Vannaman
Cover Design: Rule 29
Photo illustration by Todd McQueen: www.toddmcqueen.com

Printed in the United States of America
First Edition 2009

1 2 3 4 5 6 7 8 9 10

112108

Contents

Preface

The local church has a problem. We live in a time when many people express concern for "spiritual" things, but local churches have trouble translating that "spiritual" interest in the broader culture into conversions and actively growing Christians. Church attendance is declining. Baptisms are decreasing. Morality is spiraling downward. Society isn't improving.

So what are we as members or leaders in the church doing wrong? Perhaps our methodology needs to be questioned and challenged. Perhaps we need to return to the basics of Christianity, rid ourselves of our newest human techniques, and emulate Paul, who said, "I … know nothing … except Jesus Christ, and Him crucified" (1 Cor. 2:2). Our globe contains almost seven billion people, and if the Bible is true, then the eternal destiny of these people depends on their relationship with Christ. This being the case, we have an obligation to make sure the Christianity being modeled is true.

Why write a book provoking thought about how we "do church"? Because eternity depends on it. You, as a local church leader, will be judged by God about how you led your congregation.

Why us? Why should two guys serving at a seminary challenge evangelical churches? Because we bring a unique perspective: We have both worked in local churches, studied at the highest academic levels, and taught in a seminary setting. Most books offer only one of those perspectives. We understand the pressure of building the budget, engaging the lost in a way that changes lives, and building facilities that allow ministry to flourish. At the same time, we have read church history, studied the impact of philosophical thought, examined pragmatism, and studied churches throughout every century. Lastly, we are teaching the next generation and hear the questions coming from these future leaders. We have faced the challenges of connecting to credentialed academicians, students in training, and disengaged lost people in society.

We guarantee that *Franchising McChurch* will raise your awareness of many trends in the church of our day. You will encounter expected criticism and unexpected endorsements. By the end, we hope you will be able to evaluate church methods, think through long-term ramifications of choices, and be better prepared to one day hear those words, "Well done, My good and faithful servant."

In the process of writing the book, we couldn't help but include several personal stories. Some of those stories will be told by John Mark and others by Thomas. We tell these stories because just as Jesus used parables, stories often help us see our culture in a clearer manner. We will clearly delineate whose story we are sharing when you get to them.

We hope you will come on this journey with us. We both found it profitable and think that you will too.

Growing Waistlines in the Church Buffet Line: An Introduction to the McChurch

The Golden Arches: Big Macs, golden fries, and the best Cokes you can get are all right around the corner at your local McDonald's. Almost every country in the world has one. The sandwiches are the same; the fries are the same—this ubiquitous American institution symbolizes American success.

Dick and Mac McDonald never dreamed their small hamburger stand in San Bernardino would become a corporate giant. Dick and Mac made fifteen-cent burgers and sold them like crazy. They provided good food and fast service, but the brothers never found a successful approach to expand beyond their single burger stand until they met a salesman named Ray Kroc.

Ray sold mixers—Multimixers to be precise. This marvel of 1950s engineering was a soda jerk's dream. One Multimixer could whip five of the best milkshakes you could imagine all at the same time. Ray Kroc believed in his product so much that he mortgaged his house, sold everything he owned, and purchased the exclusive rights to distribute the Multimixer. When Ray found out that Dick and Mac McDonald ran *eight* Multimixers in their little stand, he packed his bags and headed west for California.

Ray pulled up to the tiny burger stand. He watched McDonald's employees quickly and accurately serve customer orders. About halfway through his milkshake, a dream began to percolate in Ray

Kroc's mind. What could be better than convincing the brothers McDonald to open several of these McDonald's burger stands? For each stand, he would supply at least eight Multimixers!

It was a hard sell. That same afternoon, Ray met with Dick and Mac, who were not convinced expansion would work for a small restaurant. Earlier attempts had failed. Besides, who would be crazy enough to franchise a simple burger stand? Kroc volunteered. His first store in Des Plaines, Illinois, opened in 1955, and more locations quickly followed. By 1963, the one-billionth burger was served to Art Linkletter live on American television. Kroc's dream of selling more Multimixers became one of the greatest restaurant success stories in America.[1]

Yet McDonald's success does not represent the same thing to all people. What some see as a tasty meal served fast, others see as the cheapening and devaluing of life itself. It has become common to insert the term "Mc" before a word to express disdain or to reflect that something is a cheap imitation of reality. New neighborhoods sprouting three-thousand-plus-square-foot houses become McMansions. Jobs in cubical farms are referred to as McJobs. Discarded bits of chicken are processed and formed into Chicken McNuggets. You get the idea. Even the *Economist* features an annual "Big Mac Index" evaluating the cost of a Big Mac in different countries as a means of estimating the value of a given currency.[2]

Sociologist George Ritzer noticed some of the trends back in the 1980s. As he formulated his thoughts, he eventually published what became known as the McDonaldization thesis in a 1993 book titled *The McDonaldization of Society*. Framed as a quadrilateral (more on that later), Ritzer believes his McDonaldization thesis serves as a helpful interpretive grid to understand developments in American and Western societies that seemingly dictate life in the twenty-first century. In the next few chapters we will introduce more of Ritzer's thoughts to help us understand the four aspects of McDonaldization in society and our churches.

So what is McDonaldization, and why are we talking about it in relation to the church? According to Ritzer, McDonaldization is simply the "processes by which the principles of the fast-food restaurant are coming to dominate more and more sectors of American society as well as the rest of the world."[3]

Churches unintentionally pick up on the ideas of McDonaldization through leadership magazines, conferences, and books that teach how churches can engage more of the American culture through certain structural, communication, and ministry models. But when these models are applied in the local church, it can McDonaldize, which can lead to compromised discipleship, theology, and the loss of the prophetic role of the church. In the process, McDonaldized churches become prisoners to the shifting tides of consumer culture as their leaders tend to chase "what's next" instead of "what matters."

When "What's Next" Fails to Appear …

"I just don't understand why our church won't grow!" yelled Mike McClasky, deacon at Hope Christian Church in the Chicago suburbs. Situated in the shadows of megachurches Willow Creek and Harvest Bible Chapel, Mike felt like a failure. "I have served in this church for over thirty years, and we have *never* grown above two hundred people in attendance—something is wrong!"

Mike's pastor Joe groaned. The last time Mike became frustrated with the negative growth numbers of the church, he led a charge to remove the former pastor. When Joe interviewed for the position, he wowed the committee with his understanding of the latest trends. Joe even outlined his vision and plans for the church to grow. Mike and other church leaders were elated. Now they could finally put their church on the map!

But in five years of ministry at Hope, Joe never saw an increase in membership. It seemed every family that started to attend regularly simply replaced another family that had left. The church sent Joe to conferences to get new ideas. He read all the latest ministry books. The church started cell groups, added greeters, became seeker friendly, mailed full-color postcards to the community, hosted block parties—they tried it all. But they saw no results. Nada. Zero. Zilch.

They were stuck.

Feeling like failures, Joe and Mike wondered if there would ever be a turnaround. What's the point of continuing a ministry if it is going nowhere? They could try to implement the growth strategies from the latest book, but they doubted if yet another new ministry focus would help.

Shifting Tides in the Cultural Pool

As our culture shifts from the supposed security of the modern era to the uncertainty of the postmodern, pastors and church leaders desperately search for new methods and models to extend the reach of their congregations and make inroads in their communities. Is it so hard to know how to be a church? Isn't our simple goal as churches to share the hope of Jesus with a lost and dying world and turn as many people as we can into fully devoted followers of Christ?

But we have a problem. Church leaders, theologians, and lay-people all sense that something is broken in the American church. How can we win the lost when the church is broken? Someone writes a book or article presenting a new solution almost every month, but the solutions are all over the map. Which ones will *really* work?

Worse, just like the battle over American waistlines, some churches hide from reality or act like they don't really want to fix the problem even though they know something is wrong. Instead, an intricate production of pointing fingers at megachurches, small churches, church planters, or emergent leaders begins. It's *their* fault for growing too fast or failing to grow or growing in a nontraditional way.

Add to that pressure the reality that anyone can assume the role of the critic. Blog sites, denominational papers, and even secular presses begin to pressure the church. Internal critics willingly join external ones in hurling missiles at the next overly obvious target. Been there. Done that. Didn't care for the sequel.

When we set out to write this book, we didn't want to add to the clamor of empty criticism. At the same time, we felt the need to sound a warning to churches in the evangelical community. As such, this is not a tell-all book. We don't name names unless individuals or churches are actively commenting on the issue. We simply want church leaders to think through their actions.

Our research into the phenomena of McChurches actually began by talking with local church pastors about some new trends they were experiencing directly. The more we dug into the issue, the more we realized serious problems were infecting some of our congregations. What were we to do?

We discovered that McDonaldized elements do not always translate well into the realm of the church. In fact, they may be harmful to their long-term viability. The elements of McDonaldization that initially seem so attractive (and may even produce good results when applied) frequently carry a dark side that doesn't reveal itself until much later in the life cycle of a congregation. In thinking through the issues, our concern grew as we realized that these concepts and ideas have become a part of the fabric of our church culture.

Another trend we noticed was that the churches that experience the temptations to McDonaldize more frequently fall into the "free church" category. Free churches are evangelical congregations that have little or no denominational hierarchy. The congregations regard themselves as autonomous, and while they may cooperate or network with other congregations, they maintain their independence. These churches historically maintained their autonomy and congregational forms of governance from a scriptural standpoint (you can read more about it in chapter 10). Ironically, in the process of McDonaldization, some free churches have now sacrificed their autonomy for a hierarchical structure imposed by an external congregation.

Finally, a major issue in the McDonaldized church relates to connecting creativity to content. In order to reach the American culture, churches need to be fast on their feet, looking for ways to connect and exercising creativity. But creativity for the sake of creativity is hollow. We have to back everything we do with solid content that takes people from the initial point of salvation to becoming fully devoted followers of Christ. McChurches tend to miss the greater mandate of the church, leaving a congregation full of immature believers.

Facing McChurch

As pastors, we know the church in America is struggling. Our congregations are facing overwhelming odds and circumstances. We've watched churches in our community take on more and more McDonaldized concepts and ideas only to set themselves up for failure down the road. In talking with other pastors in America, we began to sense an urgency to find a methodology to reach the next generation. Many young leaders attempting to reach postmoderns for Christ have learned that some of the methods that led to the growth of previous generations of churches have contributed to the postmodern disenfranchisement from the current church.

To help outline some of the challenges we are facing, the first four chapters of this book will introduce you to the principles of McDonaldization found within much of Western society and tie them to issues in the church. Starting in chapter 5, we will look at some of the decisions many churches are making without regard for their McDonaldized content.

At the end of every chapter, we have included a section called "I'll Take That to Go," which is a review of the key thoughts in each chapter. In addition, you also get a visit from the local church health inspector asking crucial questions that relate to your ministry and McDonaldization. Our hope is that you hear the warnings we raise in relation to the church.

The church is designed by God, instituted by Christ, and

empowered by the Holy Spirit. Despite claims to the contrary, the church is still God's designated means of reaching our world and will continue to be so until Christ returns for His bride, the church. Do we struggle? Yup. Have we messed up? Sure. Does God still want to use us? You bet!

So what's a church pastor or leader to do? We're glad you asked! In the coming chapters, we want to introduce you to the four aspects of McDonaldization that infect American society and the church as a whole.

CHAPTER ONE

Over One Billion Served:
Effective vs. Efficient Churches

I (John Mark) rubbed my eyes and did a double take. There on the billboard off of I-35 was an advertisement I couldn't believe. Emblazoned on the white background, an advertisement for 30minuteworship.com promoted a service with "you in mind." I didn't know if I should marvel at the remarkable efficiency of the church to squeeze another service into its Sunday morning routine or the fact that this congregation believes a thirty-minute Jesus fix is enough. I guess if you can get a pizza in thirty minutes or less, why not church?

The allure of a thirty-minute church seems attractive to Christians frustrated with the rut of the traditional service. Still believing that church attendance is important for their Christian life, why not consume it fast-food-style? Everyone is short on time, so why shouldn't Christians be able to consume the little bit of church they need to get them through the next week? At least it would be an efficient use of their time.

The Challenge of Efficiency

The guys working the grills flipped the burgers faster than I had ever seen. The motion was seamless—insert spatula under meat, flip the wrist to toss the burger in the air, and then press the patty as soon as it hits the grill. As demand rose, they would take one of the hot burgers and place it on a bun, allowing the next person on the assembly line to add the appropriate toppings the customer ordered. Wrapped in what seemed like milliseconds, the order was placed on the heating tray until the cashier could place it in the bag along with the fries. Fast. Custom. *Efficient.*

George Ritzer's concept of McDonaldization began here. And for good reason. Efficiency is the process of McDonaldization most of us are able to experience and quantify. In fact, consumers demand efficiency. We are unlikely to return to our local Starbucks if the baristas take forever to make a grande caramel macchiato. We expect service to be fast, efficient, and consistent. When the checkout lines at my local Wal-Mart were consistently understaffed, leading to long lines, my family willingly paid slightly higher prices at the local Target. With four young preschoolers, we wanted to be in and out right away.

Businesses are also concerned with making things as efficient as possible. It helps their bottom line. When I worked in the fast-food industry, the goal was to wait on the customers and have the food in their hands in under one minute. Our manager timed performances at least once a week and adjusted schedules, breaks, and workflow based upon what would produce the maximum benefit for the consumer (hot food served quickly usually meant a repeat customer) and for the store (more clients served in a more efficient manner equaled greater sales-per-hour margins).

People also experience this on the Web. When I purchase a product on Amazon.com or Apple.com, I have my account set up for one-click purchasing. I put items in my shopping cart, and when I am finished shopping, I click one button to buy it all. Since I set up an account with Amazon.com in advance, the company stores my information in a secure database. It reuses that data every time I click the purchase button. One click and I'm done. No worries about parking at the mall, walking to stores, or standing in line. The Internet is quick and efficient and usually cheaper.

Efficiency experienced in this manner is positive for both the consumer and the business. Efficient systems work. Our Western economies are built on it. By utilizing principles of efficiency, we maximize our profitability and increase revenues for shareholders. In business, you want happy shareholders.

Efficiency in the Church

Can the church be efficient? Should it even matter? Does the church have a clientele to impress? Do we have shareholders we want to make happy?

The short answer is—it depends. There is a sense that churches need to recognize that efficient systems can aid a congregation. You have probably visited congregations that could have used an efficiency expert to make things work more smoothly. Frequently, the use of educational space or even the order of services could be changed to maximize time and resources.

Even more so, businesspeople who serve on boards and committees will want to see efficiency in operations of the church. Were visits logically grouped to cut down on excess mileage? Is the church

purchasing the right technology to accomplish its task without spending too much? Are staff members multitasking so the church gains the
biggest benefit from the services they render? Are reporting structures
in place to give accountability for how the pastor spends his time?

There are some areas where efficiency can benefit a congregation
(easy-to-find nurseries, restrooms, information, etc.), but ministry as
a whole is not necessarily efficient. When James, the pastor of a small
church in the Detroit area, was informed by his church board that
he needed to keep a daily log of his activities, he wanted to pull out
his hair. Every day, he started a new worksheet tracking his phone
calls, visits, and time spent with people. Nathan, the chairman of
the church elder board and a prominent businessman, railed against
James' inefficiency. It was either too much time spent on sermon
preparation, too much time reading, or too much time spent with
individuals in the congregation.

"You could do so much more if you limited your time to ten minutes per person," Nathan suggested. Nathan could not understand the
world of ministry. He saw the church in terms of the business he ran
on a daily basis. Sermon preparation can take significant hours of a
pastor's time, not to mention prayer. Of course, ministry focuses on
people. Certain aspects of ministry will never be efficient if we are
to have meaningful relationships with those inside or outside of our
congregation.

One of the issues we face in regard to efficiency in the church
has to do with the nature of the church itself. Beyond buildings,
beyond the trappings of religious practices lies a reality that is often
not stressed enough—*people are the church*. When Jesus talked about
the establishment of the church, He was not discussing the property

a congregation might possess (Matt. 16:18). The apostle Paul, writing to the Colossian church, reminded them that Christ is the head of the body (Col. 1:18). Maintaining a living organism is messy business and, quite frequently, defies efficiency.

Effective vs. Efficient

If the church is designed to be God focused with reaching people as the end goal, perhaps we should draw a contrast between what is effective and what is efficient. Effective organizations work in the manner in which they were designed. They consistently produce results that reflect the aims, goals, and mission of the organization. In the process, effective organizations attain the greatest amount of production because their structures and organization work toward the stated goals of the whole.

Efficient organizations also work toward attaining results. Their production of results will reflect the aims, goals, and mission of the organization. The difference is that where the effective organization emphasizes how the organization works together as a whole to achieve the stated goals, the efficient organization strives for rapid attainment of the goals, sometimes at the expense of the totality of the organization. Even people within the organization may be sacrificed in order to attain the stated goals more rapidly or efficiently.

As you can tell, a fine line exists between effective and efficient. In the case of our churches, we are called to be effective. When congregations tip the scales in favor of something efficient, they begin to lose track of the goals and aims of building the kingdom. On the flip side, churches working together according to their stated design become very effective. Let's look at how this plays out on a practical level.

Where Effective Churches Win

Effective churches manage their resources—budgets, schedules, personnel—to accomplish the work of God in their communities without making efficiency the ruling principle of the congregation.

The relationship equation here is simply that of stewardship. How do we take care of the things entrusted to us in order to impact a lost and dying world? There are at least three areas where this matters in the life of churches.

Budget

How we spend our money relates more about who we are than just about anything else in our personal lives. The correlation remains when we talk about our churches.

Perform a simple analysis of how a church spends its resources. Churches spending heavily on staff have made that a priority. In staff-heavy churches, you usually find a couple of scenarios: (1) The church is overstaffed—perhaps the congregation hasn't been growing or is even losing ground, and the church holds on to staff positions that are no longer needed; (2) the church is staff dominated—the congregation relies more on paid leadership to accomplish its goals than on the people in the church itself. Churches *must* support their staff financially so the pastors do not have to worry about providing for their families. A church that does not take care of its leaders demonstrates a lack of faith and is a bad testimony to the community.

Some churches spend most of their resources on buildings. Whether the buildings are old and demand maintenance or the church is busting at the seams and needs a new building to accommodate growth, congregations must balance their needs and resources to avoid becoming overly committed to buildings. As stated above, the church is *not* a building. New church plants are discovering the reality that many cities and towns are not allowing churches to zone land because of the loss of revenue. They become creative, utilizing schools, YMCAs, or renting other spaces in order to have a place to meet as a congregation.

Churches must decide what to do during a period of growth. Do they start multiple services or a new building program? Do they plant? Go multicampus? The movement that seems most common currently is the multicampus setup, which maximizes the church's efficiency. While the initial technological investment may be high, overall, it balances itself out when calculating the ability to reach new people and the opportunity the satellite campus has to draw upon the resources of the main campus. Satellite campuses share staff members, budgets, office costs, marketing costs, and accounting costs. It is one of the most efficient models currently operating in church-growth circles. We will return to it later in the book.

Balanced churches maximize their effectiveness to keep the focus on the main purposes of the church. Missions and evangelism paired with discipleship are the characteristics that mark effective churches. Some stress only the missions and evangelism and miss the discipleship aspect, but most pastors would tell you that the growth of their congregation is directly proportional to the amount of resources and energy expended in reaching a lost and dying world. Again, looking at the budget of the congregation, what is the percentage of giving dedicated to reaching the lost? Budgets may look different in each church, but how much does your congregation demonstrate its commitment to the Great Commission?

Effective churches keep the main purposes of the church in focus when setting budget priorities.

Schedules

Sunday morning is the main time the church across the world meets together to worship. If a church invests time in just one service, it must be the Sunday congregational gathering. Most guests visiting a church come on Sunday morning, and we should be prepared. Careful thought must also be given to the order and flow of the music, other elements, and most importantly to the preaching.

When planning services, an effective church takes advantage of time. Awkward transitions, musical elements lacking excellence, or even announcements that ramble on without purpose convey a sense that a person's time is not important. Church staff and volunteers must work together to demonstrate the best the church has to offer to God.

It seems odd to many younger adults, but former generations demonstrated how much they cared about what happened on a Sunday morning with their clothing. Families would attend church in their "Sunday best" to demonstrate their honor to the Lord and their respect for His holiness. While the issue of formal dress may have gone out the window, the question of how we spend our Sunday morning or other meeting times is crucial. Are we careful to be mindful of the time, but still open to the movement of God? It is a delicate balancing act, but one that must be conducted each and every week.

Last week I (John Mark) visited an established church near the heart of a major metropolitan area. Talking with the pastor, I listened as he shared his concerns about the congregation God called him to shepherd. He praised the people of the little church who were making great strides in reaching out to their community. They transformed their Sunday morning rituals in order to reach out to a changing and ethnically diverse community around the church.

"The main challenge," he quipped, "is that the Spirit shows up every week and promptly leaves at noon." He started praying with the leadership of his church that the congregation would grow to the point where it was comfortable with the realities that when the Spirit of God moves, it is often not on our timetable. This means that with all our planning, we must be ready to accommodate those in whom God is moving.

In the little town of Jena, Louisiana, God broke through during a service at Midway Baptist Church. The congregation had scheduled an old-fashioned revival meeting that would meet every night from Sunday to Wednesday. On the last night of the revival, people began to repent of sin. As they repented, they began to deal with deep issues in their church. The interim pastor, Bill Robertson, believed that they needed to add another night to the revival since God moved so powerfully.

Seven weeks later, Bill brought the ongoing revival to a close. In a town famous for racial riots that broke out in the fall of 2007, no one anticipated God's grace to fall on the small country church and then spill over to the surrounding community. With more than one thousand people in attendance on the final evening, Bill and several of the pastors of other churches in the area looked over the sea of faces from every ethnic group in the community. The revival in Jena led to racial reconciliation, personal salvations, and repentance on the part of the churches. God showed up. The churches responded. "God has brought about this revival," Bill said. "As a result, people are being saved, lives are being changed forever, and a true peace has come about, bringing unity to this area like we've never seen."[1]

Seven weeks of nightly meetings? Can't be done anymore, right? *Effective churches surrender to God's timetable rather than forcing God to conform to theirs.*

Personnel

Most of the pastors, preachers, and teachers of congregations serve with honor in the roles God called them to fill. Effective churches ensure that the gifting of the staff members correlates to their ministry roles. Most churches would prefer a teaching pastor who teaches with passion and effectiveness or a worship pastor who is not just a great musician but effectively leads the congregation in worship each week.

At one church I (John Mark) visited, the worship pastor was not onstage. I found him in the sound booth. He believed that if he discipled musicians to lead in worship, he served the kingdom in the most effective manner. Recognizing his gifting as a discipler, the church encouraged his unique interpretation of the music ministry.

Effective churches catch the vision for this. If your youth pastor lost his passion for youth two years ago, the programs in place will only sustain the numbers for a limited time. Either the youth pastor needs to move on or the church needs to find a new role within the boundaries of the congregation that might reignite a sense of ministry passion in his or her life. In order to accomplish this, church staff must maintain close relationships with the lay leaders of the congregation—personnel committees, elder boards, pastoral leadership teams, etc.—so what God is doing in the individual staff member's life can be communicated effectively to the congregation as a whole.

When it comes to the issue of personnel, effective churches catch the vision for churchwide ministry. The phrase "every member a minister" reflects this. It is not the case that every member functions in the specialized call of pastor or even leader, but the New Testament picture of the church reveals heavy involvement from every member. Even the early church carried this forward. Membership in the body of believers carried a covenantal concept that ensured the active participation of the believer as part of the discipleship equation.

In some respects, Thom Rainer captured the heart of this concept in his book *Simple Church.* For Rainer, the hallmark of a true disciple of Jesus Christ is service to the body of Christ. Thus, the formula might work out that the number of mature believers in your ministry equals the number of volunteers. While there are some failures to this concept (think of the usher who simply passes the offering plate and counts the money on Sunday and uses this as an excuse to avoid the spiritual growth that happens in a small-group Bible study), some of the churches most effective at reaching the lost are those that function as mature congregations filled with volunteers with a desire to serve in any area of the church where there is need.

Effective churches emphasize the ministry roles of the entire congregation. The ability of the church to present itself effectively to the outside world directly relates to the concept of service—from the congregation to the pastor. When we work together as a body of believers with Christ as the head, we can effectively follow the leading of the Great Shepherd without chasing after the things of the world.

But as we stated earlier, there is a fine line between effectiveness and efficiency. In our quest for effectiveness, we can be carried too far and begin to emphasize efficiency. When efficiency for the sake of efficiency becomes a focus of the congregation instead of the Word of God, the church loses out.

Where Efficient Churches Lose

In the twentieth century, church-growth experts began to look at the nuts and bolts of how the church functioned. This was not an analysis of theological or philosophical *why?*, but rather a praxis-oriented *how?* Hints that America was quickly following its European counterparts into post-Christianity alarmed many experts, leading to a reevaluation of the church from the consumers' point of view. Seeker churches like Willow Creek began to ask questions like "Can visitors find the nursery?" "Is there easy access to sermons or information on the Web site?" "Can good parking be found?" While these detailed elements were not the thrust of the gospel or even what the churches were about, there was a tacit acknowledgment that the church was functioning in a consumer-minded culture and that the people who visit a church will evaluate it based on these things.

In a recent interview, Jim Henry, former pastor of First Baptist Church of Orlando, which grew to megachurch size under his leadership, discussed the challenges of growth. Because of space constraints, efficiency on the part of Henry and his staff became essential. Henry noted that if he spoke too long, those who attended the first service would not have time to move from the parking lot to let in those attending the second service. Systems of efficiency were introduced to aid with the egress of the early service. Henry timed his messages more carefully. The church gave a staff member the responsibility to cue him when time was running short. "'You begin with faith,' Henry says, and in his case at least, you end up as an expert in traffic management."[2]

Efficient churches place church systems and programs above the spiritual needs of people. Ask any pastor with time constraints on a service, and he will voice his concern that sometimes he feels trapped. With all of the things we have added to our services—special music performances, excellent worship, graphic media, multiple services, televised or broadcast services—we have to ask ourselves, "What would we do if God showed up?"

George Ritzer cued his readers on this as it related to our society as a whole, noting how efficiency keeps us from stopping to reflect or ask serious questions of others or ourselves.

Efficiency leaves no room for the enchanted. Anything that is magical, mysterious, fantastic, dream, and so on is apt to be inefficient. Furthermore, enchanted systems are often complex, and involve highly convoluted means to whatever ends are involved. And they may very well have no obvious ends at all. By definition, efficient systems don't allow meanderings. Thus, designers of efficient systems try to eliminate as many of the preconditions for enchantment as possible.[3]

Ritzer strikes at the core problem of the efficient church. With all of our time maximization, we inevitably minimize the amount to which the Spirit of God can move in a congregation. In order to get the next service started on time, the pastor has to close the service right away, perhaps without a time of reflection. People are herded from one place to another in order to accommodate the next group of attendees. In short, we miss God.

Furthermore, in an attempt to attract more congregants, many churches have moved away from the core Reformation promise of Word-centered worship. Evaluating this is quite easy. If the Word of God functions as the foundation for every believer's spiritual health and life, why do many churches spend less time studying the Word of God together than they do singing? We know. We are meddling here. But is it a valid question?

Believe it or not there are actually drive-through services, and they have been around for a long time. With the exception of non-personal television or Internet campuses, these perhaps epitomize the consumer mentality of American religion. You can visit a church without ever leaving the comfort of your own car. You can turn the radio station to the appropriate channel to hear the sermon, or if the preacher gets too loud, you can turn the volume down a little or even completely off. The Daytona Beach Drive-In Christian Church originated in 1953 at the location of the Neptune Drive-In Theater. In 1957, the church bought the property and continues to have services there. Currently you can worship in person inside the little chapel, sitting outside of your car in the shade, or in your car.[4] Andrew Kaufman from *Time* magazine has an online photo tour of the experience including pictures of the participants partaking of Communion wine in their cars and the offering being taken.[5]

The Metropolitan Community Church of the Quad Cities in Davenport, Iowa, apparently tried the same thing during a Memorial

Day service. "Just pull up in our parking lot," the pastor
the community. He went on to promise "some humor in the even-
ings. Congregants, for example, will be dressed like anglers in tune
with a fish theme."[6] According to the article, "Clowns stationed on
Harrison Street will attract cars to the church parking lot located
on West 31st Street. Drivers will be greeted by a team of three
'anglers' and supplied with the daily scripture and a take-home homily.… Everyone will be given communion, but this will be specially
delivered in a tackle box, the minister said, in a clean bait cup."[7]
Thankfully, the current church Web site does not mention any plans
to host another event of this nature.[8]

The practice of drive-through spirituality never completely
caught on, but other places have attempted similar events. In
Orange, California, the Main Place Christian Fellowship operates
a drive-through prayer booth.[9] People pull up to the small building's drive-through window where someone prays with them. This
prayer booth seems to be one of their outreach opportunities. In
fact, the creation of a prayer booth did not seem too odd for this
church, which has operated an office-supply store called Office Stuff
and a thrift store in the same shopping center.[10] All of this expansion
into nontraditional and even income-producing ventures leads one
to ask about consumerism and the church.

We are not advocating a return to the three-hour Puritan homily.
We are not even encouraging sermons of an hour or more. After all,
the mind can only absorb what the seat can endure. Pastors cannot
preach excessively long sermons and expect the congregation to continue benefiting from the material they present. Reaching that point
of no return does not happen in most churches across America. The

primary struggle with most churches comes from an opposite desire to satisfy the consumers, we mean, *congregants*, and keep them coming back. So if the congregants desire to be let out at a certain time, the speaker makes sure the service ends. If the consumer desires to limit the sermon to a specified time, the preacher prepares messages for that time limit.

By the time the pastor includes meaningful illustrations and narrative wordsmithing, time is up. Congregants face the realities of another Sunday of entertainment or storytelling and miss the very thing their souls crave—the Word of God. We are not dismissing creativity, the need for illustrations, or even the concern we should have for connecting the audience to the text, but does creativity eclipse the content of a sermon? We will talk about this a bit later.

Other pastors have maintained content, but minimized the length of the sermon. Although their motives cannot be known, perhaps the desire to keep the service short or to lengthen the praise music or other reasons have led to shorter sermons. Consider the church we mentioned earlier, 30minuteworship.com. According to its Web site, the corporate time of singing lasts only ten minutes. The sermon twelve to fifteen. At least they leave five minutes for reflection and the offering.[11] Can a pastor effectively teach any content to a congregation in twelve to fifteen minutes? Let's face facts. Many preachers stand in a pulpit week after week communicating content that probably could be condensed to fifteen minutes and be more effective *and* efficient.

The key here is the nature of the content itself. Do we craft messages that are centered on the text or focused on a topic? When we seek to communicate the Word of God effectively, the content must be scriptural. In helping the congregants wrestle with the realities of life as they are confronted with the challenges of the Bible, any reduction of sermon length that compromises the integrity of a message in order to accommodate the congregation's desire for a fast-food, efficient religious service encourages consumerism and is not healthy.

Some of those famous preaching machines of prior generations surely overdid it, right? You can remember the boring sermons, some of them read from manuscripts. The disconnected illustrations. The three points and a song. Thoughts like this send shivers down your spine.

Pastors must carefully navigate the waters, attempting to provide the needed content without speaking longer just to meet a criteria. When the job is finished, the speaker is too. A text-driven sermon discusses the selected text without chasing numerous tangents that take up time. If the pastor is following the text, he must stop when the message has been communicated. Additionally, text-driven sermons will cover the material selected. Perhaps not every word, but the main ideas and presentation must be covered in order to be text driven. The speaker communicates to the audience what the text intended to be communicated.

In stating this, we are affirming that the Bible and the text itself is what feeds the growing Christian. Experiences are neat. Singing is great and brings us to the throne of God. Drama or video may cause us to pause and reflect. But at the end of the day, God's Word is the only thing that our spirits feed on to be able to grow. The form the sermon takes reflects the pastor's respect for the text.

In the book of Acts, a pattern of God's movement begins to appear. The trajectory of the book of Acts itself is the prophetic proclamation of the gospel in increasingly greater contexts. Key to the expansion of the church in Acts is the preaching of the Word of God. When Peter and John were imprisoned and forbidden to speak of the gospel, the empowering of the Holy Spirit came upon them, and they went out to "speak the word of God with boldness" (Acts 4:31). Stephen died preaching the Word of God (Acts 7). In Paul's ministry, he stayed in Corinth for eighteen months simply to teach the people the Word of God (Acts 18:11).

It is the Word of God that allows the church to be prophetic. The Word of God contains the power we need to confront issues in our culture and society. When we lose out on proclaiming the Word and stress human wisdom instead, we are doing a disservice to our culture and we are harming our congregation. Is it hard to consistently preach biblically oriented messages? Of course! But the call of God in our lives and ministries has to be focused on the Word. We will return to this thought a bit later in the book.

The biggest area where churches can lose if they embrace efficiency as a foundation for their ministries is in their outreach to people. We have visited church after church where the impression was that you are nothing more than a number. Like standing in line at a fast-food joint waiting for your ticket number to be called, visitors can be made to feel as if there is no place for them. Sure, the congregants smile and even shake their hands, but as visitors they are "processed" through an assembly line of visitor cards and formalities, never feeling as if anyone really transcends the plastic veneer they see around them.

From the outset of the church-growth movement, Lyle Schaller pointed out that people are longing for meaningful relationships. If they don't find it at your place, they will move on. If they don't find it at several churches, they quit looking. By stressing programs above people, efficient churches can give the impression that not only does the individual not matter, but there may not be a place for someone who may not fit the programmatic molds of the church.

The only way to break out of this habit is old-fashioned human contact. Churches need to close the drive-throughs and move the people inside, where a friendly greeter listens to what they are seeking and offers suggestions—even if it is just to attend the service. Formally introduce people to one another and connect people to small groups where relationships can grow. In fact, encouraging congregants to first invite people to Bible studies instead of the church service may actually help plug people into the "nonefficient" ministries of the church first.

Beyond Efficient

Unfortunately, in a post-Christian society, does more efficiency even matter? The question is not "How long until I leave?" but "Why even bother?" Until we understand that the overefficient church does not connect people to real Christianity, but only to a fast-food version bound to increase the unhealthy spiritual waistlines of consuming Christians across America, we have missed the point. Now, more than ever, churches need to carefully evaluate where they stand. The work of the church has never been efficient because the church involves real people with real lives searching for real answers. While some people may be enamored with the quasi realities efficient churches may construct, there is a time and a day in each of our lives when we enter the valley of the shadow of death. In those days, efficiency just will not do.

DRIVE THRU

I'll Take That to Go

- Effective churches effectively manage their resources—budgets, schedules, personnel—to accomplish the work of God in their communities without making efficiency the ruling principle of the congregation.

  - Effective churches keep the main purposes of the church in focus when setting budget priorities.

  - Effective churches surrender to God's timetable rather than forcing God to conform to theirs.

  - Effective churches emphasize the ministry roles of the entire congregation.

- Efficient churches elevate church systems above the spiritual needs of people.

Health Inspector

- Does your congregation tend to be more effective or efficient? What should your church do to focus more on effective ministries and teaching?

- How do you welcome visitors into your congregation? Explain how your welcoming processes put the emphasis on people so they understand how important they are in the eyes of the church and of God.

▣   What does your congregation do to ensure that every person who joins your congregation serves as a minister?

▣   What process do you have in place to move regular attendees into ministry and service?

CHAPTER TWO

Do I Get Fries with That?:
Predictability in the Pew

It was Easter. The high point of the church year. The services at New Hope had been fantastic, and several people talked about being really moved by the music and the sermon. I (John Mark) stood in the foyer, talking to some visitors, when I felt a sharp pinch on my arm. Spinning around, I was confronted by the octogenarian leader of the women's group in the church.

"Young man!" she addressed me sternly. "*If* you are still here next year, you *will* sing hymn number 118 on Easter!" (Translation: We have been here much longer than you, and if you value your job, you will modify your behavior to bring it in line with our expectations, or next Easter will be your last Sunday, pending no further shenanigans on your part between now and then!) Unknowingly, as I planned the Easter service, I violated the predictability this woman and much of the congregation had come to know. To me, it was just a song. To the elderly portion of our congregation, that song represented Easter.

Creatures of Habit?

Humans are creatures of habit. In a McDonaldized system, citizens expect things to be consistent across the board. A Big Mac tastes the same no matter where you have it anywhere on the globe. Predictability gives birth to expectation. When those expectations are not met, consternation develops among those consuming a product. This applies to external and internal factors.

Externally speaking, in the world of the church, congregations are anything but homogenous. Even visiting two different evangelical churches on the same street will lead to widely varying experiences despite the fact they carry the same core theology. In many cases, experience dictates to church visitors that entering the doors of most congregations is a not-so-magical ride back to the 1950s in terms of music and communication. Other congregations offer a more "modern" approach, but the entertainment presented is as plastic as the attractive praise team that looks like it stepped out of a movie set.

Thankfully, no matter the presentation style of most churches, congregations include genuine believers who practice an authentic faith, and *this* becomes the continuity from congregation to congregation. The issue is connecting those faithful believers with new prospects. If predictability is such a trap, how do you move a congregation from predictability to dynamism?

Predictability matters most to regular consumers. Consider clothiers Gap in the '90s. Long famous for supplying good quality "basics" with little to no branding on the product, Gap dressed the crew on *90210* and most of us who wanted simple but durable clothing while in college or on weekends. Toward the turn of the millennium, Gap shocked its regular customer base by chasing more clothing fads, leaving its new brand, Old Navy, to supply consumers with what it once held as its core market. But Old Navy wasn't the same. In the transition, Gap lost its way, causing huge losses and forcing store closings globally.[1] Culture is a fickle thing. It changes rapidly and often more frequently than one may like.

When applied to business, the principles of predictability dictate that if you disrupt your core business, you will lose valuable clients. In the churches of America, the same thing happens. If a pastor violates basic predictability assumptions among leaders of a church, either a core group of your congregation will leave, or you will be shown the door. Simple as that.

The flip side to the predictability challenge is what we would call the replication fallacy. Corporations frequently "borrow" concepts from innovative companies that seem to be making headway in the market. Analysts will look at the business model and adapt it for their corporation with the hopes that by updating their corporate model and infusing their corporate culture, their business will capitalize on the market. This works in the corporate world quite well.

But what may work in the business world does not always translate effectively in the realm of the church. Prominent churches across the United States like Willow Creek, Saddleback, or Fellowship Church all hold conferences that regularly challenge church leaders to think in new and creative ways about the practical workings of the church. Pastors and church leaders attend and return home infused with new ideas, hoping to make some changes so their congregations can impact their communities. Unfortunately, in many cases, these same church leaders attempt to replicate the larger church *in toto* by applying the principles learned in their local churches.

Churches don't work that way. Outside of the grace and provi-
dence of God, these megachurches can never be replicated despite
the ongoing attempts by some of them to replicate themselves with
video satellite campuses. That doesn't mean that their basic principles
of church leadership or organizational structure are not helpful, but
pastors and church leaders need to carefully consider and weigh the
ideas in light of their own contexts. Because a church is composed
of a community of believers with unique gifts and abilities that cov-
enant together for the purposes of evangelism, discipleship, worship,
and fellowship, no church can ever be cloned or replicated in any
other context.

Predictability and the Church

God never intended the church to be predictable from a human
standpoint because He is not predictable. God seeks only His own
glory. If you believe that the church is the representation of God on
earth, the norm for churches should be the unpredictable—dynamic
encounters with God, movements of the Holy Spirit in the congregation, discipleship, and most astounding of all in the Word of God:
sinners coming to faith. Our God, and Christianity by inference,
defies categorization and predictability. The moment we begin to
program or "do" church in any fashion that removes the ability for
the unpredictable to happen, our expectations of predictability will,
in fact, be met.

We are not arguing for chaos in congregations, as Scripture is
rather clear: "But all things must be done properly and in an orderly
manner" (1 Cor. 14:40). That being said, our services and church
structures may actually reveal that we have forgotten that our God

created the universe for *His* pleasure (Rev. 4:11). Our only expectation should be that the almighty God desires to move in our lives personally and in the lives of our congregations directly.

While in college, I (John Mark) visited a local church that had to turn people away each week because it was too full. I decided to discover the "secret" of what was happening. If I knew that secret, then perhaps other churches could do exactly the same thing. When the associate pastor met with me, I asked him directly if the music, programs, preaching, or some other aspect revealed the true secret of how the church had grown. He slowly shook his head. "None of those reveal the secret of what is happening here," he modestly stated.

I pried for more information. I simply had to know.

"We simply believed God wanted to do something here," he said. "And then we were stupid enough to pray and ask God to demonstrate Himself in this place."

No church-growth methods.

No secret formula.

Just God proving faithful when His children pray.

As that church continues to grow, I sometimes wonder if that philosophy still supports every ministry as it once did. Regardless, God chose to move in that place.

The Power of Expectation

On the corner of Wells and Ontario in Chicago you will find a fun little restaurant called Ed Debevic's. A theme restaurant, Ed's offers '50s-style burgers, shakes, and fries with a healthy dash of roadside-diner attitude. The first time I went there, the waiter threw straws and napkins at me and tossed my burger basket onto the table as he har-rumphed off to "help" the next customer. As the waitresses jumped onto the soda counter to dance and sing "Y-M-C-A," I couldn't help but admire the restaurateur's vision for such a fun place.

But the guy two tables over did not think this was all fun and games. He started to yell at the waiter for his utter disregard for the customer. He complained that the music was loud and that the atmosphere did not encourage quiet conversation. I wanted to go over and let the guy in on the "secret" of Ed's theme, but it was much more fun to watch him fuss and fume.

This poor customer had expectations of how a diner was sup-posed to operate. When those expectations were not met, he could not see the fun going on all around him. The customer simply wanted a quiet place to have dinner. Instead, he got rude service, dancing, and general chaos—something most of us came to enjoy. He missed the point of the restaurant, and his expectations led to complete frustration.

Unexpressed expectations ruin friendships, marriages, and even family connections. You should see what is happening in churches. Expectations over preaching styles, music and worship styles, pro-grams, and other issues cause rifts in congregations across these Divided States of America. People in churches want predictability. They actually do want a regular order of worship and even want to know when to stand and sit. They—*gasp*—want tradition.

Nothing irritates many cutting-edge leaders like tradition for tradition's sake. Mere traditionalism leads to stagnation and stagna-tion leads to death, right? In part, we would agree with this. There are some long-standing traditions of the church where each congregation stands with the millions of Christians who have preceded us in the journey of faith. Connectivity to history and historical identity is one thing. Mere traditionalism is another.

Mere traditionalism puts forward practices or ideas that seemed right to a culture or a bygone era but have little or no relevance for today. The practice of avoiding the third verse in hymns is an excellent example. In the past, presumably to save time, many congregations avoided singing the third or middle verses of some hymns. This became part of the tradition of the churches. Was it wrong for this tradition to begin? No. Is it okay to move beyond that tradition? By all means. We are not talking about core theology or the Word of God here.

This is where we discover the difficult aspect of discerning between tradition and cultural entanglement. Think of the little octogenarian woman I mentioned above. She was sweet as sweet could be every Sunday. She put up with changes in her Sunday school department she didn't like. She tolerated drums and guitars in the worship service. But when it came down to her favorite Easter song, there was no room for negotiation. Her reaction was similar to what we would expect from someone dealing with outright heresy in the church.

Perhaps that's the point. Tradition creates a pattern of predictability. When those patterns are not repeated and expectations are denied, for many worshippers, it *is* heresy. For church leaders in established churches, discovering where those patterns of predictability exist becomes essential to longevity in ministry. Sadly, churches will frequently tolerate all manner of theological heterodoxy to protect the patterns of predictability they have grown to love. The essential role of the teaching ministry of the church is to connect people with the truths of Scripture. Conducted well, the preaching and teaching of the Word of God return perspective to the congregation. If church leadership hopes to move an existing church forward, carefully choosing which of those patterns to dismantle takes the skill and chutzpah of a bomb squad.

Some of the struggles we now face in the American church we created on our own by ignoring the power of predictability and expectation. Take Community Bible Church as an example. Pastor Miles Garrett caught the vision for reaching out to the youth culture in the late 1950s and created one of the first church youth programs in his state. As youth leaders sought to reach the young adults, they began to modify the standard church curriculum to reach the students in high school. In the 1970s, they began to discover Christian rock and some of the early praise music. Students visiting Community Bible connected on a deep level with the music, the passionate teaching, and the relationships they developed.

But a new trend began to surface. Many of the students Community Bible reached with the gospel did not continue at the church once they arrived at adult age. Most of the former youth checked out of the church, citing boring music and preaching along with a lack of connectivity. Those who stayed in the community tried to bring the forms of music and teaching they experienced in youth group to the congregation as a whole, only to find severe reaction against it. The church leaders were fine with that "wild worship" so long as it stayed in the youth area and did not change the way the church as a whole worshipped.

In the 1980s, some of these former youth started new churches that reflected more of what they expected in a worship service.

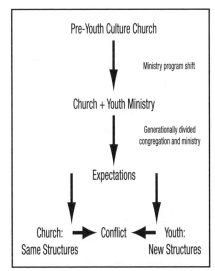

Contemporary worship became the norm. Drama and topical preaching became the rage in these churches that connected with disenfranchised former youth. Many of these churches also began to reach thousands of others of their same generation who did not know Christ as Savior, and the movement grew.

But today's cutting-edge ministry is tomorrow's tradition. Emerging churches and some megachurches began to apply concepts and ideas they learned while attending these churches in the '80s. The difference was that they attended the youth groups of these dynamic churches that incorporated the latest technology, lighting, and music into their worship encounters. As adults, these Gen-X youth were not satisfied with many of the contemporary churches of the '80s, as church services did not look like what they experienced in worship during their youth.

The pattern repeated. Many youth left the church altogether. Those who wanted to change the church from the inside out found resistance to their desires for the incorporation of new music forms, lighting, and video. They eventually left and started their own churches that reflect postmodern sensibilities, and the generational gap widened.

We are left with churches of predominantly elderly individuals with little to no vibrancy or young churches with no older congregants to offer much-needed perspective and wisdom. Our natural desire for predictability has created a generational wedge that the New Testament argues we are never to experience. How can the older women teach the younger women or the mature men instruct the younger men when these generations never see each other in worship or outside of the church (see Titus 2 and 1 Tim. 5)?

Paul clearly spoke to this issue in his address to Titus. Older men are instructed to be "temperate, dignified, sensible, sound in faith, in love, in perseverance" (2:2). Why? Because they are to "urge the young men to be sensible; in all things show yourself to be an example of good deeds, with purity in doctrine, dignified, sound in speech which is beyond reproach, so that the opponent will be put to shame, having nothing bad to say about us" (2:6–8). Notice how the defense of the church and the ability of the congregation to keep itself from external shame are directly connected to discipleship of one generation to another.

But the text doesn't stop with the men. The older women are instructed to be "reverent in their behavior, not malicious gossips nor enslaved to much wine, teaching what is good" (2:3). Their purpose for maintaining these standards is so they may "encourage the young women to love their husbands, to love their children, to be sensible, pure, workers at home, kind, being subject to their own husbands, so the word of God will not be dishonored" (2:4–5). Again, the issue comes back to demonstrating honor and glory to God. Without this generational discipleship, Paul is teaching Titus that our congregations will simply fall apart.

And what do we experience today? Our human traditions and culture divorced the generations of believers in the church leading to ossified older congregants who have forgotten the dynamics of a passionate faith while younger congregants repeat the errors of the past without drawing on the wisdom of the mature. Breaking the biblical pattern for discipleship allows a human tradition to be created that destroys the biblical plan. Recapturing the pattern of older men discipling the younger and older women doing the same is not only countercultural to the broader world but against the culture we have inculcated in many of our congregations.

When churches place human tradition of dividing the generations above God's own stated plan of multigenerational, integrated congregations, we delude ourselves into thinking our plans will bring about God's will. We are, in essence, thumbing our noses at the Creator and stating that His design is inadequate for the world today. We stress our control and place our desires over God's. In some respects this is safe. It is predictable. We know what will happen each Sunday. We can schedule our routine. The youth and their zeal won't disrupt our blessed assurance.

True life in Christ, however, is anything but routine as God places dynamic circumstances and unique people in our path every day. If the church is ready to let go of the safety of tradition for tradition's sake, perhaps revival may impact our nation again. Our expectation should be that God will move. Not that His movement should fit our predetermined boxes. If we follow His plan for the church, we should expect Him to move in our midst in a powerful way.

Replicating Predictability

The early success of McDonald's led to a string of copycat ventures, none of which could unseat the rapidly growing chain. Those trying to replicate McDonald's usually failed to get something right in the formula that made each McDonald's a financial success. Eventually groups like Wendy's and Burger King caught on that the market was big enough to accept other chains, but each company had to have something unique of its own. The genre of fast food was consistent; the rules of the game had to change in each place.

In the church-growth movement of the '80s and early '90s, churches and church leaders rippled with excitement at the rapid growth of Willow Creek, Saddleback, and other new megachurches that catapulted above two thousand in attendance. Many other congregations figured that if these churches could succeed numerically, so could theirs. They would approach Bill Hybels or other prominent leaders and ask questions about the secrets to their successes. Like the elusive secret formula for Coca-Cola, leaders couldn't seem to get the formula right to make their churches work in the same way.

Soon, these successful megachurches started offering seminars and leadership or church networks to help churches learn from the successes and mistakes of their growing congregations. Although the megachurch pastors would reiterate time and again that their ministries could not be replicated, it didn't stop some churches from trying. Pastors and leaders would clean off the book tables, snapping up every practical work on how to create effective ministries.

Churches like Willow and Saddleback became McDonaldized even further as they became the purveyors of a new batch of "consumables," ranging from Sunday school literature to multimedia, sermons to worship songs. Smaller congregations ate it up. They joined networks, deciding their former denominational ties were either insufficient or no longer practical in this new day and time. In essence, the larger churches created their own McDenominations that saturated the evangelical community with their goods, services, and brand identity.

Local churches whose pastoral staff became enamored with the church-growth movement were often at a loss. What were they supposed to do? Church leadership styles changed from congregational to CEO models. Predictable patterns in worship they had known changed overnight. Churches split. Pastors lost their jobs. Congregants began to fear change even if that change was what might sustain the church for the long term.

Many local church pastors forgot several things in their attempt to build the next megachurch with their flocks of fifty people.

1) Size does not always equal success. We will talk about this in the next chapter.

2) Pragmatic solutions to issues are frequently localized. Often the rapid growth of certain congregations has more to do with local cultural elements and the way the church chooses to address them than anything else.

3) Staff can never be replicated. Many successful churches have incredible senior staffs that possess skills and abilities that few people in any generation do. God chooses to use those gifts surrendered to Him to leave a mark for the kingdom. *Every* pastor has a unique set of gifts! God gave you those gifts so you can minister precisely where He wants you to be. That may mean ministry to a church of fifty, five hundred, or five

thousand. God knows what He needs for the progression of the kingdom. You are part of that plan.

4) Attempting to replicate ministries is a slap in the face to the God who created and gave each church individuals who possess gifts and talents to create. Sure, there is no need to reinvent the wheel, but if you don't take ownership of the programs and ideas you import, you violate the concept that your members have gifts from the Holy Spirit designed for the building up of the congregation. Before you import something, see if God is leading you to create something new from within your congregation.

5) God is the one who builds the congregation. Church leaders should be faithful to do what God commands us to do. We should preach the Word, evangelize, disciple, and lead. If we are faithful to His commands, let God build His church!

Avoiding Predictability

Predictability is a trap that can lead to staleness in our ministry. It teaches us to rely on our own strength and methods instead of expecting God to move powerfully in our midst. Patterns of predictability offer a false sense of security that ultimately fails when the pressures of life appear.

But how do we avoid this trap? It is as simple as "trust in the LORD with all your heart and do not lean on your own understanding. In all your ways acknowledge Him, and He will make your paths straight" (Prov. 3:5–6).

We know. It's a simplistic answer. But is it really? Everyone has a plan for *your* church to be successful. They market the latest solutions for evangelism, growing your small-group ministry, or touting the latest conference. Their solutions range from complete overhauls to minor tweaks to get your congregation in line. Sometimes their advice is good. Sometimes it leads you down the wrong path.

Here is the key issue: It is not *your* church. It is God's. Surrendering to His plan of church growth (evangelism and discipleship) is hard to improve upon. The extent to which your church accomplishes the aims clearly laid out in Scripture is the extent to which your church is truly successful. Like the Pharisee in Jesus' parable (Luke 18:9–17), too frequently we pursue our own glory and worldly success, not caring about the glory of God.

If the glory of God is our focus, we would spend more time discipling congregants who live like the world instead of like Christ.

If the glory of God is our focus, we would spend more time in prayer and less time studying the latest methodologies.

If the glory of God is our focus, the pastor's personal evangelism would increase to the level expected of the congregants.

If the glory of God is our focus, we would seek to end worship at the altar of human traditions and plead with God to destroy our predictable worlds so that He can reign in our hearts and over our churches.

God has called you to shepherd His people. Rise to the challenge of your unique flock of sheep. Follow the Great Shepherd unfailingly.

DRIVE THRU

I'll Take That to Go

- The Predictability Principle

  - Unexpressed expectations are a danger to the health of the congregation.

  - Mere traditionalism locks churches in an unhealthy cycle that ignores the lost.

  - Today's cutting-edge ministry is tomorrow's tradition.

  - Multigenerational worship is essential to function biblically.

- Replication Fallacy

  - Size does not equal success.

  - Pragmatic solutions to cultural issues are typically localized.

  - Staff cannot be replicated.

  - Attempts at replication ignore the unique gifting of the Holy Spirit.

  - God is the true builder of the congregation.

- It's not *your* church!

Health Inspector

- As a church leader, to what extent do you simply maintain the status quo in order to avoid rocking the boat?

◻ How do the discipleship ministries of your church reflect the multigenerational mandates of Scripture?

◻ If your church offers multiple services with differing worship styles, how do you keep from effectively dividing the congregation you serve?

◻ What trends in attendance do you notice between the services (if you have more than one)? Which aspects of the services are based upon mere traditionalism, and which focus on scriptural and historically significant ideals?

◻ How do you discern between mere human tradition and scriptural guidelines?

◻ What safeguards are in place for you as a church leader to check the methodologies you read about or hear about at conferences against Scripture before implementing them?

CHAPTER THREE

Supersized for the Kingdom: Counting the Numbers

"Most churches, pastors, and laypeople measure success by looking at the three Bs: buildings, budgets, and bodies. The more you have, the better you must be doing." Expressing his frustration with the measurements of success in ministry, pastor Jim Pannell could not have put it better.

Pastors and church leaders want their congregations to be successful. After all, this is our calling—to expand the kingdom of God. Pastors work tirelessly to grow people so they, in turn, win and grow others. The hope is that the cycle begins and doesn't stop. It's in the pastor's study where men fall on their knees in frustration as the growth they work toward doesn't happen. Should his members simply head to the nearest megachurch since he can't compete? Is the church just wasting time and energy? Was accepting this ministry a good investment of the years he spent in seminary?

Counting the Cost

Almost every investor is concerned about his or her ROI—return on investment. With high-risk ventures, a high rate of return is possible. With low-risk ventures, often the return is smaller but more secure. We all want to make sure those things in which we choose to invest will pay off in the end. Businesses perform cost analysis reviews to find weak spots in their corporate environment. International companies like GM retool their entire organization to maximize their investment. Layoffs or plant closures are announced, or restructuring upsets the executive applecart. The end goal: more profit for the shareholders.

Calculability deals with numbers. These numbers, when talking about the church, represent people—or so I have been told. Success in ministry, as in business, is often relegated to either this measurement or the financial one. Buying into the "Bigger is better" mentality, churches often reflect the dominant culture in this regard. It is almost natural to assume that a church that reaches ten thousand in attendance is much more effective than the church of eight hundred. Or that the church with the three million dollar budget is more significant than one that barely reaches its one hundred thousand dollar goal for the year. But are these items truly helpful in analyzing the effectiveness of a congregation or a ministry?

In a telling article by T. D. Allman in the March 2007 *National Geographic* titled "The Theme-Parking, Megachurching, Franchising, Exurbing, McMansioning of America," today's megachurch is analyzed much like any other theme park or alternate-reality entertainment venue in the Orlando, Florida, area. "The Megachurch is the culmination," writes Allman, "of the integration of religious practice into the freeway-driven, market-savvy, franchise form of American life."[1] In the article, Jim Henry appears as the vocal spokesperson for church growth as calculability. "We've done what Wal-Mart and football have," Henry told Allman. "We've broken down the idea that 'big is bad.'"

When is it right to apply such standards of calculability to the church? To be sure, numbers matter to God. We are told about the five thousand who show up to hear Jesus speak and how the two fish and five loaves fed the whole crowd. Simply opening the pages of a Bible gives you a book called Numbers ... but we digress. Numbers and calculated averages help us identify trends in culture and in our local church. We should measure certain things regularly to examine key markers of growth in a congregation: How many salvations, baptisms, and new church members were there last year? Can we set achievable goals for the coming year? A marked difference exists, though, between wisdom in how a church operates (budgets based on numbers and giving records) and allowing God to provide miraculously. In many instances, leaders insistent that all the numbers simply "work" to cripple congregations.

In Scripture we are reminded of the problems of being too numerically minded. David's insistence on carrying through with a census had dire consequences. Likewise, basing our ministries on calculable factors removes key elements of the role of God working in the midst of His people. George Mueller and other examples from history might be called as witnesses to argue that God is simply seeking to honor His name by providing miraculously for the actual needs of His children.

Mueller, an evangelical concerned about the plight of orphans in England during the nineteenth century, established an orphanage designed to address an overwhelming social problem. His original vision was simply to care for the orphans in his own neighborhood. But in just over a decade, Mueller was overseeing an amazing ministry with more than three hundred orphans. Twenty years later, that number expanded to over two thousand orphans, one hundred fifty missionaries, literature distribution, and schools.

Mueller determined from the outset that God would provide for every need without taking on debt. Even more radical, Mueller decided that if God provides, only God needs to know about the need. The result: Mueller never asked anyone for a dime. Stories about how he would sit the children down for breakfast without having any food in the kitchens were common. As they would bow and pray for their daily needs, someone would knock on the door and ask if they could bless the children with food for that day.

The central key to Mueller's success was a simple reliance on God as provider. His numbers never worked. Too many kids, not enough resources, and a God-sized vision resulted in ministry that few people today would have the passion to pursue. Mueller discovered the simple lesson that God will frequently provide for His children in ways that are beyond our expectations.[2]

However, not all of the means by which God provides are found in numbers. As frail humans, our means of measuring success too frequently relate to the numerical sphere. Meet with a group of church leaders. To size up the people around them, the question of, "How many members do you have?" or "How many do you have in attendance?" is so predictable that it almost reaches the category of ubiquitous. Of course, once the number is established, the questions often turn to budgets or building programs or number of campuses. While there is nothing wrong with these questions in and of themselves, the problem becomes where our focus lies. Usually these types of questions can lead to pride on one side or self-defeat on the other.

The hard truth: *God cares more about the holiness of a congregation than He does the size of the congregation.* Using numerical benchmarks to somehow size up the blessing God pours out on a congregation or to evaluate members' ability to stay faithful to the guidelines of Scripture lacks spiritual maturity and reveals our reliance on human understanding in our vain attempts to build the kingdom of God through our own methods.

In the book of Acts, God strikes Ananias and Sapphira dead for lying to the Holy Spirit. In 1 Corinthians 5, Paul commands the believers to put away the evil from themselves. Churches best display the glory of God when they reflect the holiness of God, and they best demonstrate a difference between God's way and the world's way when they do not look just like the world. Some churches are large not because of God's blessing, but because the pastors preach what the people want to hear or offer programs that fulfill the felt needs of congregants. Paul states that this will happen in 2 Timothy 4, when he says that people will not endure sound doctrine but those with itching ears will heap up teachers for themselves.

Consumers and the Church

At this point consumerism reenters the discussion. James Twitchell, professor of literature and marketing at the University of Florida, recently evaluated the role of consumerism and the church. Twitchell and other researchers believe that American Christianity has reached the point where churches have commodified religion, making spirituality a product to be consumed instead of a life-altering way of life. Churches that grow are those that are able to catch the market at the right time, leading to "buy-in" by the religious consumer who is less interested in theology but more concerned about personal experience.[3] The more the overall experience suits the religious consumer, the more likely that person will join with a particular congregation.

Twitchell argues that few "real" conversions take place in these churches. Instead, there is simply a static set of people who are interested in consuming religious items. Thus, free-market principles dictate that whatever congregation can attract the free-radical consumers is the one that can claim the most conversions. Thus, the most market-savvy congregations employ strong pastorpreneurs who not only visioneer the possible future of the church but also meet cultural demands in the preaching, the type of music selected, and broader appeals to the segment of the market targeted by the church.[4]

Why would Twitchell use such harsh terms to describe the process of church growth? He has no dog in the hunt. Twitchell refers to himself as an *apatheist*, an apt handle for many young adults. Apatheists are those who simply don't care about your church or religion in general. They don't see a future in religion, nor do they care if it continues to exist. They express *apathy* toward the whole situation relating to God.

Should churches listen to Twitchell and the growing voices of secular dissent on the consumer church? We can recognize their bias, but what they have to say is just as damaging because it strikes so close to the truth that many of us have ignored or bypassed in pursuit of the short-term numerical growth. Many churches simply caved in to whatever process, whatever program, whatever *worked* to get people in our doors. We justify it based on the claim that we can show salvations or our number of attendees grew. We then publicize our growth numbers to our denomination or networks. The more growth, the more publicity. The more publicity, the more the church's "stock" rises in the court of perceptions in the evangelical subculture.

The church's Great Commission from Jesus Himself is that we are to *make disciples*, a process that does lend itself at times to the principles of church growth. Part of real church growth entails moving beyond the basic teachings of Christ to the enjoyment of the meat of the Word and the replication of the life of each believer by making more disciples.

We have heard pastors state that their churches teach only the basic things to attract people to the faith and that they expect converts to move on to other congregations as they mature in their faith. By definition, this means their congregation is *not* a church, but rather it is an ongoing evangelistic meeting. Unfortunately, many of the trappings of the church lite/evangelistic group cannot be replicated in other congregations, yet this is what these converts expect. When they seek out a church in which to grow, they either learn to die to themselves or become like the seed tossed on the edge of the road that springs up quickly but dies off even faster (Luke 8:4–7).

Numbered among the Faithful

So how do numbers factor into this? Our evangelical subculture prizes fast-growing congregations as evidence of God's blessing and congregational health. While God may choose to grow some congregations and that growth may happen with solid, biblical discipleship as part of the event, this tends to be the exception rather than the rule. Many congregations feel such pressure to grow numerically that when the growth doesn't happen, they settle into patterns of defeat.

When did God stop using small churches? He didn't. But when church fashion moved from evaluating churches based on their faithfulness to God's Word and His principles of growth, the shadow of many larger congregations (and scores of mega-wannabes) began to loom across the evangelical landscape. What was the small church to do? As a committee in a small church once suggested to our pastoral staff, "We should use our reserve funds to bring Franklin Graham to our congregation to preach! Once he preaches here, people will see how great our church is and stick around!" Even for lay members of congregations, the pressure of being "the next big thing" in church growth can begin to evidence itself in faulty reasoning and unscriptural behavior.

Whatever happened to a Gideon approach to church growth? Looking over the valley where the Midianite armies camped, Gideon's leaders and men were nervous about the possibilities of success since their army numbered around thirty-two thousand and the Midianites were "as numerous as locusts; and their camels were without number, as numerous as the sand on the seashore" (Judg. 7:12). The troops were restless. How were they going to win?

God gave the solution. Send home anyone who is afraid. Twenty-two thousand left. Gideon found his army paired down to just ten thousand. God still wasn't happy. Using a leadership evaluation tool—the "how you drink water" personality test—Gideon found himself with only three hundred men.

How idiotic! Everyone knows you have to match the strength of the armies man on man to have any hope of winning! Gideon should have used growth strategies of creating multiple military camps under his leadership to help swell the ranks. Perhaps if Gideon could have brought more men on board by using the latest in recruiting methodologies, they could have outnumbered the Midianites in manpower if not in technology. What was God thinking?

God was thinking about His glory. Gideon and his three hundred men followed God's direction to the letter. You could almost feel the adrenaline surging through their bodies as they crept up to the edge of the Midianite camp. One of the Israelite lieutenants made a nervous joke to mask his fear. This would be the last time he ever lapped water from his hands!

Once in position, the men waited for the signal. There it was! The men pulled their clay jars off their torches in a smooth motion. As they threw their pots on the ground, the resounding clash threw the enemy into confusion. Raising their trumpets to their mouths, they blew a victory note. "A sword for the LORD and for Gideon!" they cried in unison (v. 20).

The enemy camp plunged into turmoil. Confused, the Midianite soldiers attacked each other. Those who fled left the scene quickly, but not before Gideon got word to some of the other leaders of Israel to stop the enemy from retreating. By the end of it all, Gideon, his army of three hundred men, and then the other tribes and communities of Israel together experienced an amazing victory.

Who really procured the victory that day? God. Using low-tech weapons of torches and clay pots, trumpets and loud shouts, those three hundred men routed the entire army of Midian. Why has the church bought into the lie that only big churches can win in the battle against our culture? What victory is it if we accomplish an incredible feat with massive budgets, slick advertising, targeted marketing, and the newest programing? Do we miss out on the greatest experience of God working through the "least of these" to impact all of eternity when we spend our efforts more on marketing tactics than prayer? In fact, some of the great movements of God in history have come from small churches that decided to get right with God. As He moved in their midst, their small clay pots, torches, and trumpets become the sharp swords God used to bring salvation to hundreds if not thousands.

God wants to work through the small and unexpected so that He gets the glory. We are convinced that the future hope of revival in America stands with the pastors willing to give God the glory, faithfully administering the Word of God to their people, and letting God work miraculously in unique ways. This is the desire of virtually every pastor, but somewhere along the way a desire to reach people caused some to focus on the latest techniques and marketing tools. Perhaps we have gone too far and need to return to a simpler form of church, presenting the pure gospel and watching our miraculous God work through His people. This may mean large numbers. It may not.

At Fuller Seminary, Finnish theologian Veli-Matti Karkkainen added his international perspective to the concern that many Western churches focus unnaturally on numbers.

Industrialization was built on the ideas of specialization, effectiveness and calculation and so the church amidst that culture was also dominated by the same sensate ethos. Even though the principle of standardization so poorly fits the dynamics of church life, it was imposed. Furthermore, the focus turned from local communities to central headquarters, since they are more easily managed and pressed into a uniform mold. Finally this imitation of the ethos of industrialization led to synchronization, concentration and maximization. What can be counted and managed is what matters; the number attending church services, the amount of offerings, the size of buildings and so on.[5]

Investment Guidelines

Thousands of investors each year increase their wealth by investing in the latest growth company. Dabbling in the stock market and their diversified portfolios, they add to their own personal bottom line when the fortunes of the companies they invested in rise in a hot economy. Things do change in companies from time to time. Hostile corporate takeovers, changes in CEO, employee satisfaction, and public reception of certain goods can change personal wealth portfolios overnight.

What if there were a market that traded in church futures? What if your church decided to go public and become the latest

IPO offered for sale? Would you invest? What signs of growth could you offer that would make your church appealing to other investors? Do you have regular growth, consistent baptisms, and a strong children's ministry? How's your youth program? Can you reach the aging boomer population?

We hope this sounds ridiculous. The church is not a business; its pastors and leaders are not CEOs. The gospel is not a commodity that can be bought and sold, no matter how you want to package, market, or sell it. The church is not designed to be a purveyor of good feelings or emotional experiences like some kind of amusement park or vending machine. We can state all of this, but the reality is that many churches evaluate themselves by asking the same type of questions mentioned above. Do the people have buy in? Are our ministries cutting edge? Do we utilize the best technology? Are we growing numerically?

At the end of time, your congregation will stand before God. He will evaluate your ministries according to the hallmarks of success He put into place for the church, not human inventions. In fact, God's investment strategy is often exactly opposite to the measurements of the world. Take the following as an example:

1) In Matthew 28:18–20, Jesus concentrates on the main mission of the church—making disciples. Thom Rainer asked a very apt question in his book *Simple Church*: "How do you know you have made a disciple?" Some ministries stop at conversion. Some want to push a complex system of catechesis on the new believer. Jesus spells out the measurements we are supposed to note: Make disciples by bringing about (a) the baptism of new believers and (b) teaching them to observe everything He

commanded. Based on this passage alone, we could expect a successful church to be marked by baptisms of new converts and increases in spiritual growth and maturity, as believers are taught the Word of God and then replicate this process.

2) The book of James talks about true religion being practiced when we care for widows and orphans (James 1:27). In the midst of all the programs and outreach your church conducts, who runs the orphan ministry? Who sees to the needs of widows? Can we honestly expect God to bless our churches when this basic concept is ignored in many congregations?

3) First Corinthians 3:2 and Hebrews 5:12–13 chastise the people of God for their failure to thrive on the deeper things of God. They rejected the meat of God's Word and wanted only the basics. The author of Hebrews tells the congregation that many of them should already be teachers, but they reject learning more about God and simply settle for the easy, palatable things.

This list could go on, and we will talk about other issues later, but the key point is that God had a plan for His church. He told us how He would evaluate it. He promised to protect it. He even called the church His bride, whom He is waiting to redeem. He loves the church and wants to redeem it, contrary to all the books that seem to indicate the concept of "church" is out of fashion and not viable anymore. God's plan for the future *is* the church.

We need to make ourselves clear on this point. We are not criticizing megachurches. God alone can judge their effectiveness. The crux of the issue is that the size of the church does not matter. If your church is not following the teachings of Scripture in your congregation, you cannot expect the true blessing of God. A large number of attendees at a church may simply point to good music or preaching not to real depth on the part of the average member, something shepherds of all congregations will have to give account. Large numbers of attendees in a congregation may also mean that the pastor or other church leaders are teaching what people want to hear. In so doing, they rob their congregants of true spiritual growth. Positive messages may sell, but the Bible also stresses judgment, a theme we too often forget about. Small churches, large churches, medium churches—every church faces evaluation of what God thinks of it. Where does your church stand?

DRIVE THRU ⬆

I'll Take That to Go

- ▢ God does not measure success by the size of your congregation so long as you are focused on the things God called the church to do and to be.

  - Size does not always mean God is blessing a church.

  - Lack of size does not always mean God is displeased with a church.

  - Size is not an indicator of spiritual growth or maturity among attendees.

- ▢ Calculability is a human trap that distracts us from the real aims of the church, like evangelism and discipleship.

- ▢ Humans cannot produce God-sized results.

- ▢ God is the ultimate judge of a congregation and its true health.

Health Inspector

- ▢ What God-sized risks has your congregation taken after significant prayer?

- ▢ How do you prevent your ministry from being numbers focused?

- ▢ How do you prevent your self-worth as a pastor, teacher, or church leader from becoming wrapped up in the trap of the worldly model of success?

- Are you jealous when God blesses other congregations? Why or why not?

- Would you be willing to downsize your ministry if called to do so?

CHAPTER FOUR

Have It My Way: Control and the Church

Henry Ford had an amazing idea that changed manufacturing for-ever. Give a guy one focused job to do, and he will do it better than if given multiple tasks. This idea birthed the assembly line. Instead of a small team of two or three people building the whole vehicle, the assembly line worker could easily participate in a large "team" as an integral component in the manufacturing process. Quality improved, and cars were produced much more quickly. In essence, Ford's utilization of the assembly line created a new level of quality control that revolutionized an entire industry.

Control factors as measured in terms of McDonaldization help provide the basis for efficiency, calculability, and predictability, but they have a big drawback. The more systems or technologies exert control, the less we participate and control. This is one of the more insightful observations in George Ritzer's thesis. The big trade-offs humans make for efficiency, calculability, or predictability may remove elements of individual control.

Take that worker in Ford's plant—we'll call him Frank. Let's say that Frank's job is attaching the steering column to the vehicle. Day after day, Frank dutifully does his job. Monotonous as the job is, Frank enjoys the sense of pride he has because he is part of Ford Motor Company. His work is important because no one else can attach the steering column like he does nor has his experience.

Just last week, however, Frank got a pink slip. Ford decided to replace Frank, the human person who might assemble the components with 90 percent accuracy, with a new robotic arm assembly that produces 99.5 percent accuracy and doesn't require a pension. The pride in his work and sense of contribution that Frank possessed disappeared. The company may have made a great choice that was efficient (more cars more accurately), calculable (the output of the machine could be adequately measured), predictable (the machine is designed to produce the same results every time), and controllable (machines don't picket or join labor unions). The expendable part of the equation was Frank. His self-worth suffers as he realizes that a piece of machinery could do everything he did and more, without sick days or overtime pay. Frank begins to question if the company only viewed him as a machine someday to be replaced by Frank 2.0—the robot.

In our churches, issues of control are an ever-present reality. The internal politics in any given church structure produces more than enough fodder for a detailed sociology experiment. The concern we face in many of our churches is the exertion of control structures that ultimately dehumanizes those in the congregation. If the church of Jesus Christ is composed of individuals working together, who is in control? The pastor? The elders? The deacons? The committees? The people? What does it mean to shepherd a flock?

During the growth of the megachurch in the '80s and early '90s, books discussing the role and leadership of the pastor became common. In many cases, these leadership books were much-needed resources. Some pastors failed to challenge and lead their congregations to address the issues of the day. Other pastors needed basic leadership skills simply to bring unity to their congregations. New images from the business world began to infiltrate the churches as more people sought to find better ways of describing the role of the pastor.

CEO Leadership

In many of these resources, pastors were encouraged to function as a chief executive officer, making the key decisions for the church. If churches resisted such strong leadership, the pastor might consider planting a congregation that reflected his own personal philosophies of ministry, including a strong-pastor-as-CEO model. Centralizing the authority around the pastor had benefits—better control of the "product" of the church. Services, ministries, music, and preaching could all center on the main leadings of the pastor without going through committees or other leadership teams. In addition, those not happy with the pastoral leadership could be encouraged to seek community elsewhere.

As the CEO, it became the pastor's duty to bring things into shape—to bring growth to the church's bottom line. Many churches reorganized around this concept, and as a result, members of congregations took less of an active role in the life of the body and waited for the pastors or the staff to lead out before getting in line.

Complicating issues, growing churches noticed a natural correlation between the size of a congregation and the leadership of the staff and pastor. In smaller churches, the church conference or business meeting is a necessary component of accomplishing the work of the congregation. Projects need completion, financial realities must be discussed, and issues concerning the life and health of the congregation often come to the fore. These smaller churches function as a family to discuss issues from the lease of a new copier to the salary of the staff. While some of these meetings look more like World War III and less like the church, the reality is that the smaller the congregation, the more directly the individuals in the pews are involved in the governance of the church in places adhering to congregational polity.

The larger a church grows, the less congregants control directly. The staff or key church committees make major decisions. The larger in size a congregation becomes, the more control becomes centralized under the pastor and the staff or elders of the church. A breaking point emerges around five hundred congregants, which naturally creates demand for the staff to take on greater responsibility. The congregation is no longer able to handle the day-to-day affairs of the congregation directly, and the control shifts. While the congregation will still be presented key issues on which to vote, the congregational meetings become fewer as the demands for effective leadership from the pastor and pastoral team increase.

But "pastor as CEO" is not the scriptural image presented of the pastor. Instead, Scripture offers the challenging image of the pastor of the church as a shepherd. In fact, the term *pastor* is also translated from Greek as "shepherd." The author of Hebrews described Jesus as the Pastor or "Shepherd of the sheep" (Heb. 13:20). The standard of a pastor is that of Christ, not business leaders, no matter how well the methodologies appear to work.

Observe the role of the shepherd out in the field with his sheep. He cares for each of his sheep and knows each and every one. In fact, he knows when even one goes missing. He protects them against the weather and predators. He corrects them and trains them. If a pastor in the modern age follows the role of pastor as CEO, can he accurately live up to this expectation?

Unfortunately the presentation of pastor as CEO reflects the McDonaldization principles of control. The pastor as CEO must exert control, which is accomplished best when the church operates with efficiency, calculability, and predictability. Just as in any business, the pastor possesses absolute authority to reorder staff, encourage new building projects, and dictate the budget. If all goes well, growth will occur, usually measured in terms of numbers. If the pastor cannot generate growth, either his methodology needs to be changed or the CEO should be removed and replaced with a more-effective leader. As this concept continues to morph in the latest trends of church growth—multisite churches—issues of control become even more apparent out of necessity.

Control and Multicampus Congregations

Multicampus congregations represent a philosophy of outreach that allows congregations of all sizes to extend their ministries beyond a centralized location. Multicampus strategies take a variety of forms, from video venues to cultural campuses (Hispanic, black, or white congregation sharing the same budgets and buildings but meeting at separate times). Some multicampus services share the same order of worship and message; others rotate teaching pastors between campuses or provide separate worship venues reflecting a wide diversity of style preferences but sharing the same sermon.

The advent of multicampus ministries brings new focus to the issue of control. Multicampus congregations embrace the concept that they are one church in multiple locations. The format typically centers on a strong main campus with multiple branches within a geographical range, allowing the congregation to reach farther into other communities. Sometimes churches locate these satellites within the same city. Other congregations plant these campuses in other cities or even other states. Churches of all sizes are experimenting with multiple campuses.

The starting point is moving to multiple services. No matter how we stage it, each worship experience we create takes on its own identity. Any church worshipping in more than one service creates more difficulty displaying the fellowship, or *koinonia,* characteristic of the church in the book of Acts. The multicampus structure follows different ecclesiastical structures, but in almost all cases, the more campuses, the more control is exhibited from a small group of leaders.

Many times the staff becomes the centralized board of directors with the pastor as CEO. As the church grows through multiple campuses, this becomes even more important as the logistics demand stringent control factors in order to replicate the experience at the main campus. More often than not, the centralized power for the congregation shifts almost entirely to the pastor and those closest to him in the hierarchical structure.

One major factor for this is that the pastor is the one constant in every venue. Whether the church markets the pastor or the congregation itself, the pastor becomes a central element of the congregation and externally represents the brand of the congregation. In our post-denominational era, churches are more frequently associated with the name of the pastor over ties to a denomination.

The irony cannot escape the more careful observers. The vast majority of congregations utilizing multicampus strategies could be categorized as "free churches." Free churches emphasize independence from outside denominational control, elect their own pastors and leaders, and typically practice some form of congregational church polity whether it is elder led, committee led, deacon led, or pastor led. Churches that participate in hierarchical church structures like the Episcopal Church typically do not own their buildings or have much of a say in who is going to serve as the leader of the congregation. The denomination makes those decisions for them.

In these multicampus churches, the pastor as CEO becomes like a bishop in an Episcopal structure. The bishop (usually with a council) hands down decisions to be enacted in the congregations under his or her authority. The congregants can either affirm the decisions by their continued attendance or leave the church. There is little room for input.

In most multicampus structures, the campus is simply a branch of the main congregation, so all decisions are ratified and maintained by the pastor and the leadership team. Instead of being an autonomous church that owns its own facilities and practices the New Testament model of submitting to one another in Christ, they are subjected to the external control of a centralized business structure.

Offerings taken at the satellite campus are deposited into the main campus's accounts, and the bean counters there determine how much goes back out to meet the needs of the satellite. While this is efficient and provides for cost sharing, the ramifications are huge. Your local congregation has zero control. In function, the multicampus church is like a hierarchical McDenomination that dictates what each franchise must do.

Not everyone sees this as a problem. Hierarchical churches have been around since at least the third century, but the multicampus application of this hierarchical structure is new. It takes free churches and divorces them from their heritage for the perceived benefit of the larger corporate structure.

What remains to be seen is what will happen during a change in leadership. Since the pastor's presence helps define the church "brand" in these McChurches, when he retires or resigns, who will take his place? When one man is broadcast to all of these congregations, will his sermons simply carry on in perpetuity? Should he pick his successor and attempt to impress the church DNA onto him? When does one begin the process of transitioning in new leaders? As these churches invite more and more congregations to unite with them and become centralized under the leadership of one man, are there other issues we need to consider? We will talk more about this in later sections.

The Challenges of Control

According to Ritzer, the control factor frames the final portion of the fence of McDonaldization. Those inside the boundaries have difficulty finding a way out. Trapped inside the walls of McChurch, congregations chain themselves to the demands of a consumer culture. In order to keep up the calculability and meet the demands of predictability, the congregations are forced to become more efficient and sacrifice people on the altar of success.

At the C3 Conference held annually at Fellowship Church in Grapevine, Texas, Ed Young Jr. challenged the pastors and leaders attending the 2007 event to take control of their staffs. He advocated matching passion with position that could lead to some interesting ministry positions–skill set matches. He talked of walking into a staff meeting in 2006 and unilaterally handing out new assignments. The youth guy became the worship pastor. The worship pastor was switched to discipleship and so on.

For Ed Young Jr., he matched ministry passion with actual ministry position. This laudable action took bravery and decisive action. But not everyone commands his staff with the charisma of Young.

What about calling? What if our calling is to a ministry that we may not even like, but God wants us to work through the issues and challenges? As a staff member or even a layperson in a congregation, what would you think of a pastor unilaterally changing the staff composition of your congregation? In the pastor-as-CEO McChurches, you can expect more choices that challenge your calling at the expense of the expedience of efficiency. Those in control wield absolute control.

Lord Acton, in a letter to Bishop Creighton in 1887, issued the famous dictum "Power tends to corrupt, and absolute power corrupts absolutely." He was echoing the sentiments expressed by William Pitt, the Elder, a century earlier, cautioning that unlimited power ultimately corrupts those in possession of absolute power as they seek to maintain control. Control is a dangerous thing. That's why God created the church with a system of checks and balances to keep any from falling prey to illusory grandeurs of power.

After all, who is in charge of the church?

If you answered the pastor or some iteration of this, you just failed your ecclesiology exam! Run straight to Ephesians 4 and 5, read thoroughly, and try again! *Only Christ is the head of the church.* He is the one in control. Our attempts at human control express our own inadequacies and our own failures. As we seek to tightly control what happens in the congregation, we begin to humanly manufacture spiritual experiences.

Not only is Christ the head of the church, but He also created it and promises to build it. For our friends who gather to worship and study God's Word but avoid the term "church," we wonder why the hesitation. We know the church has a justified bad reputation because of the internal corruption, hypocrisy, and rampant spiritual failure.[1] But George Barna's recent argument to get rid of the church and its practices altogether does not carry the weight of Scripture.[2]

Who instituted the church?

Christ.

Who made the church the "bride of Christ"?

God the Father.

Who seals the church?

The Holy Spirit.

The God-ordained and Trinitarian pattern is the church! We can call it a community, a cultural gathering, or anything else we want. The reality is that Christ instituted the church, and we cannot improve upon what the Creator instigated.

Have we lost sight of what the church is supposed to be?

Perhaps we have adapted cultural practices through pragmatic desires of reaching people and then slapped a Christian label on it. No wonder we have some Christians following a simplified, easy Christianity that doesn't get close to the image presented in the New Testament. By turning the gospel into a commodity to be possessed and the church into the big-box store where we sell and purchase our spiritual wares, should we be surprised people are turning away from the gospel? It is no longer transformative, prophetic, or truly relevant to a lost and dying world. It looks and feels cheap and plastic. A quick look at the package shows that it comes from some other place, and we see that side effects could occur from eating the lead in the glossy paint on the veneer.

Postmodern Management?

The dream of many in the tech industry for years now has been the open-source movement. From Linux to Wikipedia to Open Office, people from across the globe find ways to contribute and work together to create radically decentralized programs that work. Ask a die-hard Linux user about the advantages of RedHat or Fedora, and they will overwhelm you with the problems associated with the McDonaldized systems found on Macs or Windows machines. Success within postmodernism often comes through decentralization and giving up control.

What confuses us is that for all the talk of ministry in a post-modern, post-Christian culture, the multicampus, franchised, McDonalized church appears to be another effort of the modern church to remain relevant. The cultural success of the multicampus church runs counter to the supposed needs of postmodernity by avoiding authenticity, allowing for anonymous contact, and not stressing relationships. After all, how authentic can a pastor be if he never shows up in your church except via video?

Surprisingly, despite the shift in the dominant culture to post-modern principles, elements of McDonaldization continue to prove resilient against the onslaught of postmodern ideology. Two research-ers fascinated by this trend examined the elusive elements of barbecued rib joints. Many of the best rib joints are located in out-of-the-way locations with questionable cleanliness. But just one taste has you hooked! The perfect sauce, the right amount of smokiness in the tender meat, and the best fried okra you ever sampled leave you craving more.

It's harder to find these types of food outlets anymore, which is what prompted the research into barbecued rib joints in a post-modern culture. Postmodernism heralded a shift in culture to the unique, specialized, and indigenous. Hoping for a renaissance of localized businesses that maintained a global perspective, the world could free itself from the fast-food, one-size-fits-all focus of culture. Postmodernity promised a society embracing the unique, special-ized, and local instead of the mechanized, easily accessible, and commodified.

Instead, the prepackaged, franchised, McDonaldized restaurants continue to dominate the landscape. What these researchers discov-ered was that despite the postmodern turn, a continuation between modernism and postmodernism allows adaptable modernistic struc-tures to continue their profitability and growth.[3] Think *Starbucks*. They took a postmodern phenom—the coffee shop—along with the community and local environment, and effectively translated it to a consumable product and made billions.

Could the same be applied to the numerically growing congregations across the United States? Given the current trends in postmodernism, one would suspect that we could witness the rebirth of the small church catering to the local community in ways only a connected congregation is able to do. With the exception of some emerging churches, this has not proved to be the case. In fact, the opposite seems to be true as larger churches and their modern structures continue to dominate the landscape. Is their era over?[4]

If the McDonaldization thesis applies to modernity, what of the postmodern context in which churches presumably minister today? John Drane, professor at the University of Manchester, quickly caught the power of the McDonaldization thesis as it applies to the Western church. In his Anglocentric volume titled *The McDonaldization of the Church: Spirituality, Creativity and the Future of the Church*, Drane critiques the church for embracing modernism as revealed in its existing models.

In the midst of a growing spirituality in broader culture, Drane fears that "we seem to have ended up with a secular Church in a spiritual society."[5] Drane, who correctly identifies the latent principles of McDonaldization in the foundation of Western culture, believes that the hope of the church will come from embracing a postmodern worldview that eschews the trappings of modernity. This postmodern solution would embrace creativity and stress relationships, something that Drane believes is best illustrated in his wife's clowning ministry. The question must be asked that if postmodernism is the true societal shift that some, like Drane, have been predicting, will the church be the last institution enchanted by the siren song of modernism?

The danger in posing the question—a question at the heart of every pro-postmodern ministry book—is that it assumes postmodernity as "other." In other words, postmodernity is described as the new kid on the block instead of a full flowering of the conceptual ideas of modernism itself. The brilliance of George Ritzer's quadrilateral theory points to a fairly obvious issue for the church: *Even with the onset of postmodern society, the modern still resonates.* Many of the proposed postmodern shifts within society and the church are not unlike stylized "postmodern" architecture that frequently is nothing more than a thin facade hiding a very modern building.

Since most successful business models only artificially apply postmodern concepts, Ritzer seems to indicate that postmodernity is simply modernity writ large. So, while elements of culture do reflect postmodern ideals, the McDonaldization of American culture has not changed. Big Mac lovers rejoice—the Golden Arches will not disappear tomorrow. The sociological research and theories presented by Ritzer seemingly reinforce that postmodernism is not an "other" to be feared, but rather it is a modulation of the same enchanting song sung by the same tempting sirens. The question of how the church can break the spell has yet to be discovered.

The initial promise of postmodernism for the church focused on the return of smaller, missional congregations that not only shared the love of Christ but also deepened people in their walks with Christ as they sought authenticity on their spiritual journeys. From the presses that churned out a new pro-postmodern tome every week to pastors and churches that sought to capture the essence of pomo culture, the reality has been much different. Most postmodern churches are nothing more than their modern counterparts with different dress and music. For the seemingly postmodern churches that experience numerical success, the principles of McDonaldization usually lie right below the surface, waiting to be uncovered. From strong control right down to calculating growth curves, it's all there.

Instead of franchising a branded version of Christianity, churches should rediscover the scriptural form of decentralization: church planting. We understand that some of these churches consider their campuses as church plants in a community. If the main campus controls all the events of the satellite locations and forces the preaching of the main campus pastor via video, there is no decentralization, and it should not count as a church plant. It is simply a franchise of the main congregation. Churches that plant other churches with the DNA to plant other churches will have a long-term ability to reach greater numbers of people. Sure it costs the "birthing" church. Sometimes it even tallies costs that aren't recuperated for some time, but the pattern of the early church was to plant. In a postmodern context, can we get back to the decentralized, church-planting movement that turned the ancient world upside down? There is no better time than now.

But enough about the framework of McDonaldization. You should be able to spot the four categories by now and have perhaps found ways that these infiltrate your congregation. As we turn to the next section, the focus will shift to more practical areas of ministry and how your church can break free from McDonaldization.

DRIVE THRU ⬆

I'll Take That to Go

- ▢ McDonaldized systems lend themselves to strong hierarchical control.

- ▢ The greater the number of attendees, the less control is in the hands of the congregants.

- ▢ Decentralization through planting autonomous churches is the antidote for McDonaldized systems of control.

- ▢ Christ is the head of the church.

Health Inspector

- ▢ What are the key differences between leadership and control?

- ▢ Who controls your congregation? The pastor? A deacon or elder board? How do you ensure the final authority is Christ?

- ▢ What influences a pastor to take the reins from the congregation and assume the role of CEO? How does the biblical principle of the priesthood of believers fit into this model? Does it?

- ▢ Should church bodies have more or less control over congregants? Does this leave room for church discipline?

Areas[6]	Outcomes	Negative Effects
Efficiency	Speedy checkouts, drive-throughs, streamlining	Impatience, frustration, distraction
Calculability	Bang for the buck, rankings, scores, making the numbers work	Unhealthy competition, fudging statistics or numbers
Predictability	Scripted interactions, consistency, Disneyfication	Plastic human interactions, shallow personal relationships
Control	Mechanized labor, designer babies, automation	Humans viewed as machines. People begin to view others based on the ways they benefit them.

SECTION TWO

Eating while Driving:
Theological and Practical
Ramifications of McChurch

CHAPTER FIVE

Chicken McWhat?:
The By-Products of McChurch

I (Thomas) have a friend who helped plant a church in North Carolina. The church start has boomed. The staff leads vibrant worship, and the church continuously reaches new converts for Christ. The church seems like the perfect church. But the other day, my wife began to discuss with one of their leaders what the church's government looked like. The next question concerned the doctrine of the church. The response was, "We don't want to get bogged down in controversy or doctrine of that nature. We just want to reach as many people with the gospel as quickly as possible." This phrase demonstrates the sentiment of many churches across America. Let's just reach as many people as possible with the gospel as fast as possible. I too have this desire. It's a noble concern and a reasonable guide for ministry.

I visited another church that focused on theological depth.[1] The church insisted upon a plurality of elders, congregational government, baptism by immersion, expository preaching, and even family worship. They desired for all kids to attend the main service and worship with parents and the elderly. The church members genuinely seemed to care for each other and pray for one another. This church body seemed healthy. Upon further investigation, I discovered that new additions more frequently came from transfer of membership than from evangelism and that baptism most frequently was of children already in the church family. While this church contained meaningful membership and a healthy theology, it seemed to lack the evangelistic zeal present in the previous church.

These two churches represent the extreme cases. You can work your way in from that point, finding churches that focus on either (1) reaching as many people with the gospel as fast as possible, (2) building a healthy church that equips believers for works of service, (3) or some combination of those two principles. Maintaining this balancing act is difficult. To invoke the latest church-growth techniques, one often compromises theological principles. However, a church too inwardly focused can result in a lack of focus on evangelism.

We do not desire to critique either side of this issue too harshly. Both goals are noble, biblical goals. We do, however, wish to provoke thought in pastors of these congregations to consider how well they maintain the balance between theological integrity and consistent evangelism. How do you reach people with the gospel in our time? How do you inspire believers to fall in love with Jesus and grow in the depth and meaning of their personal walks with Him? How do you accomplish both at the same time? These are the questions of our churches. The answer lies in a balancing act that nears impossibility. We must acknowledge that attempts at correction sometimes swing the pendulum too far one way or the other.

This is what we see happening in the current situations of church movements. The seeker-sensitive movement recognized a lack of evangelism that had taken place in some of our inwardly focused churches.

These seeker churches accomplish a great goal by reaching out to lost people and being sensitive to needless barriers to the gospel. Perhaps they removed a few too many, but they did attempt success at principle number one—reaching as many people with the gospel as fast as possible. This resulted in Billy Graham crusades every Sunday morning. The congregations contained shallow believers, but at least they were believers.

One reaction to this movement comes in the emerging church, which has noticed a lack of community and openness in larger or seeker-focused churches. These emerging models emphasize being authentic and real with human struggles while maintaining a smaller-community feel. In an even further reaction, several new house-church movements have sprung up. A few churches even encourage house churches and treat them as small groups. The desire for community and openness constitutes the reaction to the size and anonymity present in large seeker churches. Leaders like Mark Dever and his Nine Marks ministry encourage churches to focus on meaningful membership in light of the overinflated roles and lack of discipline associated with some churches.[2]

The challenge for the pastor of the local congregation is not to give into pressure for increased numbers by pushing theological principles to the side. A pastor who can balance (1) reaching as many people with the gospel as fast as possible and (2) building a healthy church that equips believers for works of service has accomplished the work of a good and faithful servant.

We do not claim that the list that follows is all-inclusive; however, it should help spark thought about your current situation and help you consider ways in which you may find the proper balance between too inward focused and too outward focused. We also do not think churches possess all of one side or the other. Some are positives and some are negatives on each side. Again this list should be used simply to evaluate your current situation and where you may fall by looking at specific examples that may lend to one focus or the other.

Two Extremes of Church Life	
Too Inward Focused	**Too Outward Focused**
Focused on believers	Focused on the lost
Deep theological preaching	Simple gospel message every Sunday
Like a theology class in seminary	Billy Graham crusade every Sunday
Believer oriented	Seeker sensitive
Koinonia, community focused, small groups	Larger groups; anonymity is okay
Church discipline practiced	Member absenteeism is tolerated
More attendees than members	More members than attendees
Tendency to use church words: "Jesus in your heart," "soteriology," "born again"	Tendency to avoid words like *hell*, *blood*, *crucifixion*, *sinners*
Worship in buildings (with steeples)	Worship in nontraditional building (mall, storefront, school, and no steeple)
Entire congregation worships together	Multisite church is the newest technique
Expects members to evangelize	Expects members to bring lost friends
Equipping believers for service	Preacher convinces the lost to accept Christ
Services three times a week with weekly visitation programs	Services one time a week; staff visits those who request it
Sings the doxology while holding hands	Has a band that sounds very similar to secular music
Sings the old hymns with an organ	Rock band with a guitar and drums
Congregational music	Professionals sing while congregation listens
Success determined by spiritual growth and love of the congregation	Success determined by growth in the numbers of the congregation
Pastor visits shut-ins and hospitals	Pastor manages staff, focuses on preaching and evangelism
Ministers to widows and orphans	Has few if any widows or orphans
Members mixed in age range and socioeconomic status	Members similar in age range and socioeconomic status
Some church members do not want growth; not as friendly with visitors	The church has designated greeters, ambassadors, and other visitor-friendly emphasis
Run like a family business; congregation has more input	Run more like a corporation with a CEO or board of directors

This list is similar to a list of restaurants, which we are much safer to identify than naming various churches. At one end of the spectrum, you have a fine-dining experience like Ruth's Chris Steak Houses. At the other end of the spectrum you have McDonald's.

The fine-dining experience could come in the form of a family-owned restaurant or a chain, but it will have the expected characteristics of other fine dining. For example, linen napkins are a must. The consumer experiences the meal with a highly trained wait-staff and expects to be there for at least an hour. This establishment's survival comes from the experience and connections. The customers pay far more money in order to eat at this place. To them, it is worth it. If the atmosphere and experience lose value, then the customers transition to somewhere else.

McDonald's contains its own set of challenges and impressive elements. The money comes from a high quantity of customers flowing through the doors. The profit margin results from cheap food served quickly with expected results and familiar atmosphere. The napkins are always paper, and in more recent times, new contraptions even limit the number of napkins that can be pulled at one time. The food is portable, and time is of the essence.

Most people eventually experience the transition from McDonald's to fine dining. Some even find this transition difficult. During the first few minutes of the meal, the setting may be uncomfortable. Instead of the plastic utensil that came with your fast food, there is real china, multiple glasses, linen napkins, and two forks on the side and another placed at the top. What are you supposed to do with more than one fork?!

And the time! Who would have thought that someone would spend three hours at a meal with multiple courses? Even the food itself comes out in tiny servings that look more like modern art than something edible.

With time, you adapt. You begin to appreciate the service of the waitstaff. You start to cherish the handcrafted art of the local chef who knows just how to bring those flavors together. You learn what the glasses are for and what to do with all the forks. What may have been uncomfortable at one point in your life becomes the very thing you crave later on.

Is There a Choice on the Menu?

So which is better? We would imagine that a balance somewhere in between would work well. You don't need to eat fast food every day, despite the fact that some could. You also can't spend half of your life at the dinner table, eating food that looks too pretty to touch and, in many cases, looks better than it tastes.

This experience can be applied to churches as well. We have been to churches with a more liturgical style that did not provide a friendly atmosphere for visitors or children. Where a manuscript was read poorly and church roll was taken before the doxology was sung while holding hands.

But we have also been to very healthy churches where the preacher read an expository message from a manuscript in captivating fashion. We have seen the staff strategically plan each prayer, the music leader plan each song to accompany the sermon, and the service last well over one and a half hours. We found ourselves enjoying this deep theological experience and learning about meaningful membership. Utter amazement filled our souls when the congregation remained another twenty minutes to talk with each other. The church had only one service and directed latecomers (after the church had filled to capacity) to other nearby healthy churches. Those who wanted to join the church had to attend a Friday night and Saturday morning new-members' class, where the leaders explained everything about the church and a good bit about Christian doctrine. This may be the healthiest church we have ever visited. What a magnificent experience.

We visited a self-styled regional church that had services at 9:00 and 11:00 with Sunday school starting at 10:00. If the Spirit moved, He better do so in the proper time, just like the workers behind the McDonald's counter. The massive facility had parking attendants directing you to the proper location. If you turned on your lights, you parked in the visitor section. (We suspect poor attendees could do so and never be caught!) Well-trained greeters stood outside the facility, and all spoke the same line.

What we didn't know was whether to feel like royalty or like a cow being led to the slaughter. As we watched all the other attendees, we felt more like the latter. The service had been maximized for time. We couldn't believe what they crammed into fifty-five minutes. No announcements, the short prayers beginning before the music even stopped, and special music began immediately upon the "amen" of the offertory prayer. The preacher's topical sermon entertained us all with a two-minute tear-jerking video clip. Not a dry eye in the place, and then almost as suddenly, the service ended. Of course, the service repeated the exact same way one hour later. During the invitation a person walked down front and joined the church in five minutes with everyone voting to approve the person as a member.

We have also seen magnificent facilities where greeters made you feel like an honored guest. A place where the pastor knew your name before you ever arrived at the welcome desk. The music was professional with quality musicians, the sound superb, and the lighting perfect to set the mood. The preacher demonstrated commanding delivery with poignant stories that brought the message to life. Passion exuded from musician and speaker alike. In addition, two people accepted Jesus as Savior during the invitation. We left feeling excited about the passion demonstrated and the professionalism, which indicated they took God's work seriously.

So which method is better? Many of these possess good and bad characteristics. While some are healthier, others reach more non-Christians with the gospel. Here lies the rub. Why is it so difficult to have a healthy church and many new converts to the gospel?

Organizational Decisions—Theological Consequences

Imagine in your mind a theological continuum. On one side of this line would be a church maintaining theological integrity and a healthy focus on evangelism. Toward the other side of this slide rule would be churches that are approaching a dangerous level of consumerism and becoming what we call a McChurch. As you begin to move the slide rule across various decisions made frequently in churches all across America, various theological principles would be violated. In order to help spark discussion and thought about how simple organizational decisions have theological consequences, let's examine a few of the theological principles and the decisions that may compromise those positions.

The Meaning of *Ecclesia*

Many decisions taken for granted in today's churches potentially compromise the meaning of the term *ecclesia*. The word *ecclesia* is the Greek word most commonly translated in the New Testament as "church." The word mainly means "assembly" and primarily refers to a local, visible assembly of believers in Christ. So decisions that compromise the "gatheredness" of the congregation can potentially harm the meaning of the church.

The first decision that would begin to compromise the church in this way would be the move to have an overflow room with video. Such rooms, while providing extra space, compromise the gathered congregation. While in the context of the larger discussion this addresses, such a decision seems tame. But it is at this level that organizational decisions begin affecting theological principles. A church may affect the "assembling" of the membership even further by moving to multiple services. This move might be temporary while a larger auditorium is built, or perhaps having multiple services is the long-term plan for growth. Either way, both of these decisions have in essence created multiple congregations meeting in one facility. While the church may assemble together on Sunday nights or Wednesday nights when the crowds lessen, the entire body will rarely, if ever, meet together. This provides no opportunity for the membership to demonstrate the care, concern, or even knowledge of another's existence, which should accompany the fellowship of the local church.

By choosing to have multiple services with different worship styles, a decision has been made that separates the congregation even further and reinforces consumer-driven mentality. The congregants can have church their way with either hymns or contemporary-style worship. Rather than learning to appreciate the taste of other members, they think individually and make consumer-based choices.

Consumer Mentality

Many popular decisions occurring in local churches may unknowingly reinforce the consumer-driven mentality. The first of these would be services that neglect corporate singing. While few find this problematic, it creates passive worship and reinforces the congregation as consumers rather than participants. We should attend church in order to give and not to consume. Thus, we go to give money, sing praises to the Lord, and engage God's Word. Each congregant should actively participate in worship. Once a band, choir, or special musicians lead out while the audience listens, the active service becomes a passive experience very similar to a concert. Consumers choose which concert to attend based on preferences of music, and churches cater to the entertainment-driven consumer mentality.

For churches that offer different styles of worship on one campus, the church consumer makes a choice based on musical preference and schedule. As will be discussed later, families may show up to church together, separate depending on preference, and not see each other again until the services have concluded. Supporting this level of consumer choice may affect our view of authentic Christianity. Is it my perspective or God's truth that matters? Can you consume worship any way you want it, or do you come to God to have your life changed?

A final and more radical application of the consumer mentality in "doing church" is the Internet church. This allows the individual the opportunity to virtually attend church without ever leaving the comfort of home. While many find this odd, those who seem attached at the hip to their laptops or iPhones may find this comforting. They work all day on computers, they sit with a computer by their chair at night, they maintain contact with friends through the computer, and they worship God through their computer. If you don't believe that this makes sense to many, then you should visit the virtual world of Second Life, where churches such as LifeChurch.tv have virtual campuses resembling the real-life versions.[3] While researching the world of Second Life, we spoke to many who claim they attend church only through this virtual campus. When we inquired, "Do you go to real church?" These "avatars" were offended because to them this was real. "It's all a matter of perspective," they told us. We fear that decisions such as these will lead to an entertainment focus, a consumer mentality, and an individualized religion.

The church of the third millennium finds itself amid a culture that has become "nothing but a meeting place for individual wills, each with its own set of attitudes and preferences and who understand that world solely as an arena for the achievement of their own satisfaction, who interpret reality as a series of opportunities for their enjoyment," as theologian Veli-Matti Karkkainen comments. These churches operate as if their "last enemy is boredom" instead of the anti-Christian dominant culture itself.[4]

The consumer-driven church may offer multiple locations for convenience. This movement, known as the multisite revolution, will be discussed in chapter 8. These decisions range from having a second campus in the same town with the ability to meet and vote on the main campus to virtual campuses where no opportunity exists for the congregation to ever assemble at one time. The decisions vary from a limited plan of one or two additional locations to campuses all across the nation with centralized control located on the main campus.

Decisions, Decisions

Our decisions have consequences. Decisions concerning the order of service, the prayers in a service, whether the congregation sings, and what to do about growth problems, all have consequences that impact the church. Churches may make decisions in the spur of the moment that communicate an unintended message to the congregation. If nothing else, perhaps this discussion will emphasize the importance of every decision in the local church and the need to think through the theological implications of those decisions. In the remainder of this book, you will see many of the popular decisions addressed along with their consequences. Our hope is that this discussion helps you think through the issues before the moment of decision arrives and that ultimately the church becomes a better display of God's glory.

DRIVE THRU ⬆

I'll Take That to Go

▫ The church must focus on reaching people with the gospel.

▫ The church must focus on creating mature followers of Christ.

▫ A difficult balance must be maintained between evangelism and discipleship.

▫ Practical decisions such as multiple services or multiple locations have theological implications, such as creating more difficulty in developing fellowship.

▫ Passive or overly entertaining worship encourages a consumer mentality among the congregation.

Health Inspector

▫ Do you have disengaged members who rarely participate? If so, how might the structure of your service reinforce or challenge this behavior on a weekly basis?

▫ How might multiple services or locations harm your ability to be "one congregation" that shares one another's burdens as commanded in 1 Corinthians 12?

▣ What steps has your church taken to challenge every member to present the gospel?

▣ What steps has your church taken to equip members for works of ministry?

▣ Has your church focused on one aspect of being the church while neglecting the other? How can you avoid this?

CHAPTER SIX

Another Milkshake, but Where's the Beef?: Sugar or Sustenance in the Teaching of the Church?

The Multimixers that Ray Kroc placed in every McDonald's continued to churn out honest-to-goodness milkshakes for years. The recipe was simple: Take a couple of scoops of ice cream, add some whole milk, and then let the Multimixer do its trick. The process was messy and required a lot of dishes to clean up, but the shakes were just right!

But it didn't take long to find another, more efficient means to produce milkshakes. What if the milkshake mix was blended in a remote location, then packaged and placed in soft-serve ice-cream machines? McDonald's stumbled into a genius idea! Now the shakes could be consistent in their texture every time (predictable), they weren't a mess to make (efficient), and the new supply method provided precise measurement of ingredients (calculability) and delivery (control).

In the 1970s, McDonald's changed its formula to make the milkshakes more like malts, leaving many customers unhappy. During this period, the milkshakes became simply "shakes" on the menu board in order to reflect the change. The change in texture appealed to some, and McDonald's kept it around. Because of the thinner texture of the shake, McDonald's even began to use a yogurt-based product to make the shakes less offensive on the nutritional charts.

But the milkshake won out. Based on customer preference surveys, McDonald's eventually switched back to a whole-milk-based shake. Menu boards changed again, returning the milkshake back to its rightful place. Despite the high-fat and caloric elements of the milkshake, the public seemed to want the real stuff.[1]

The Evolution of the Sermon

During May 2007, I (Thomas) went on a thirteen-day tour of Korea, preaching thirty-two times to more than thirty-five thousand people. As I visited these various churches, I kept hearing about this great church known as Yoido. Pastor Cho's portrait hangs in many churches in Korea, and he seemed to be a religious rock star to the churches of the region. The more places we visited, the more I wanted to attend what is considered the largest church in the world. With numbers circling as many as seven hundred thousand members, my expectations were unrealistic. I came to find out a few balloon-busting facts.

First, I discovered that Dr. Cho did not preach his own sermons. Steve Sjogren quotes Cho as saying, "Honestly, I have never given an original message in all my years of ministry here at Yoido Church. Each week, I preach word-for-word messages from either Billy Graham or W. A. Criswell from Dallas First Baptist Church. I can't afford to not have a home run each weekend when we gather. I don't trust my own ability to give completely original messages."[2]

The moment of preaching in Protestant congregations is the high point of the worship service. Everything leads up to the teaching of God's Word. But instead of carefully crafting a sermon with the true needs of the people at heart—needs that can be met only by Scripture—the focus switched. Lacking the creativity to come up with sermons week after week, preachers often turn to various suppliers for help. The Internet provides these resources for the preacher in a neatly prepackaged system. With each download, the preacher greatly increases the pastor's time to do "real" ministry (efficiency).

At the same time, the perceived quality of the sermon increases even if the pastor no longer spends hours in preparation (predictability). High-quality sermons flow each week from the preacher's mouth, and the resource pool for new sermons seems endless (calculability). This also establishes control as pastors can rely on those he feels are more educated than himself. To top it all off, he can obtain better resources for the content, including videos to accompany the sermon, putting the pastor in control of the Sunday service without spending much time in preparation.

Best of all, the congregation never knows that the pastor has replaced his personal study of God's Word with reliance upon resources. If congregants notice at all, their comments only encourage the preacher by stating what a great sermon they heard. The worse fear is that some preachers resort to entertainment-driven sermons to keep the congregation returning. Shorter sermons, less controversial content, and more entertainment will likely increase crowds. The results are measurable by the number of people in the pews. The people in the pews do not detect that the preacher no longer mentions the original languages, discusses the commentaries he read this week, or mentions the depths of human depravity. The sermon has lost its central element, and no one has noticed.

In this chapter, we will explore and expand upon how consumer-driven mentality and the McChurching of America have compromised the preacher's integrity and jeopardized the message of the gospel itself.

Preacher as the Consumer

The modern-day preacher has become a consumer of sermons. While the consideration and intake of other preachers' sermons can be helpful, the problem arises when preachers' consumption and production too closely resemble one another. Although we may think modern technology created this problem, we contend that it has only brought it to light and exacerbated it. Back as early as the 1800s sermons were printed each week in the religious newspapers. In 1935, L. R. Scarborough addressed plagiarism in a book titled *My Conception of the Gospel Ministry.*[3] Perhaps the most famous preacher to have his sermons reproduced there was C. H. Spurgeon. These sermons, eventually bound in books, have no doubt been preached in some form throughout pulpits across America and Europe.

During the 1800s the bivocational preacher lacked time for sermon preparation and relied upon the religious newspapers of his day for help. Whether these sermons were used merely as resources or preached word for word is impossible to research, as the records of bivocational preachers do not exist. Modern technology has allowed listeners for the first time to have both access to their preacher's recorded sermons and, through the Internet, access to the sources used in development of those sermons.

The preacher's consumption of sermons occurs in at least three ways. The first would be the research of passages of Scripture. This is a legitimate consumption. Preachers often consult commentaries that explain the exegetical insights and nuances of certain passages. The authors of commentaries write in a technical style that does not lend itself to oratory. Preachers rarely footnote the commentary from which the information originated because it produces an awkward effect on delivery.

A second type of consumption comes in the form of illustrations. Preachers pay money to access illustrations online or through books focusing on the topic. In addition to consuming through these mechanisms, pastors' conferences and conventions often provide venues for consuming illustrations. This type of consumption in itself is not detrimental. When consumption of information provides an inner well from which the preacher draws, along with the Spirit's guidance to highlight important exegetical truths, then consumption is positive.

The third form of consumption is the sermon itself. One may download, purchase, or listen to sermons from the greatest preachers of yesteryear at the click of a mouse. As we write this work, Thomas has his iPod full of Jerry Vines' sermons, and John Mark has his iPod full of John Piper's. Every preacher should listen to and learn from great preachers. But your content must come directly from your study of the text and your relationship with God. Don't use another's sermon. There are those who disagree.

Steve Sjogren, founding pastor of the Cincinnati Vineyard, sees nothing wrong with using content from another's sermon. He begins his argument with a story.

A friend of mine in Cincinnati was recently dismissed by his church's board of trustees because of this. As I predicted to that board of trustees, the size of that thriving church has been cut in half, the momentum they had been experiencing has gone away, and they are in big financial trouble. What a needless waste of God's momentum that had been resting upon them.[4]

We wonder whether the momentum created came from God or from a consumer mentality among the congregation. Furthermore, if the momentum resulted from a movement of God, then we doubt very seriously that a few elders could stop it. Consider the words of Gamiliel in Acts 5:38–39 (NKJV): "And now I say to you, keep away from these men and let them alone; for if this plan or this work is of men, it will come to nothing; but if it is of God, you cannot overthrow it—lest you even be found to fight against God."

Sjogren argues that pride compels us to be original in our message and that we must overcome this sense of pride. While we need to overcome pride, it comes from wanting to be known as a gifted communicator and not from wanting to be original. Thomas Long from Emory University in Atlanta agrees. He "believes plagiarism can come from a clergyman's desire to be 'sizzlingly entertaining,' and from vanity." Long continues, "Our churches have turned into theaters and our preachers have turned into witty motivational speakers with high entertainment value."[5]

These issues are not new. L. R. Scarborough, the second president of Southwestern Baptist Theological Seminary, wrote on the subject of "Ministerial Danger Signals" in 1935 and addressed three items relevant to this discussion. On commercialization he stated, "When we put the dollar mark on our ministry we forfeit the respect of high-minded men and sell ourselves at prices far below our value."[6] Of sensationalism or entertainment he said, "A head-liner preacher will sooner or later be a dead-liner preacher.… It thrives on excitement and demands so much more each time that the preacher cannot meet the demand and soon he fails."[7] He also addresses plagiarism and the lack of study as other danger signs stating, "To appropriate other men's sermons without acknowledgment and credit is ministerial littleness and spiritual thievery.… A lazy preacher deadens the pulpit."[8]

Sjogren claims that many of his favorite communicators, including two who serve as pastor of churches running ten thousand plus in attendance each week, often preach sermons with 70 percent or more content from someone else. Some of these sermons are word for word. He advises preachers to stop being original and take from the handful of truly gifted communicators in our generation. Perhaps he refers to communicators like Bill Hybels or Rick Warren, who are sometimes referred to as "mega-ministers."[9] As Rick Warren says, "If my bullet fits your gun, then shoot it!"[10] The Internet contains discussions of "principles for preaching others' sermons."[11] The results of this action could be as Sjogren describes: "In our desire to give 'killer messages' we are dishing out something far less. Think about it for a second: If you really were giving a killer message each week, would your church be the size that it is right now?"[12]

Consumerism in the pulpit exists with preachers who admire and wish to be like another gifted communicator. In this desire, they borrow in large quantity the material of their favorites. "The Rev. Brett Blair, owner of sermons.com, says anyone who buys from the trove of anecdotes and 6,000 sermons is paying for the rights to the material."[13] Thus, many see nothing wrong with preaching the material on the site. Consumerism has also taught us that a growing business is a healthy business and that if the church doesn't grow, then the pastor is doing something wrong. So preachers imitate the pastors of large churches. They preach their sermons, desiring the same result. In our minds, we forget that God has designed us for different-size congregations, different ministries, and to relate to different types of people.

Newspapers and Web sites everywhere discuss the problems with plagiarism in the pulpit. *World Magazine* carried an article in April 2005 titled "Word for Word: Religion: More and More Pastors Lift Entire Sermons Off the Internet—but Is the Practice Always Wrong?"[14] You can find discussions of dismissed pastors in the *New York Times*.[15] Even the *Wall Street Journal* discusses sermons taken from the Web in an article titled "That Sermon You Heard on Sunday May Be from the Web."[16] Willow Creek has also recognized the problem with an article titled "Plagiarism in the Pulpit: The Epidemic Very Few Are Talking About."[17]

Problem Number 1: Where Does It Stop?

As authors and theologians, we try to look at the big picture and see implications on the future of the church and theology. Our perspective lends itself to objectivity since we are neither promoting nor defending our own actions. Look for a moment at the end road of the information superhighway called "preacher consumerism." If we were businesspeople and noticed that the person we paid to preach on

Sunday mornings simply accumulated material from other preachers without tailoring it to our congregation, we would question what we were paying the preacher to do.

Taking McChurching to the next level, we would do away with the preacher. Why not simply video a better communicator into our service. Perhaps Bill Hybels, Rick Warren, Jerry Vines, or John MacArthur could be displayed on large screens. We can even do a series that flows from one great preacher to another, thus combining only their best material in order to have the best possible preaching. After all, the guy who preaches for us (we'll call him the delivery boy) often messes up the delivery, whereas the real developer of the sermon would not. Video reproduction would create better control and predictability. Or perhaps we'll just hire a part-time actor who is good at reading scripts. He can download the manuscript, work on it a few days, "preach" it on Sunday, and we'll pay him half the money with a better delivery. D. A. Carson said in a critique of plagiarism, "The substance of a stolen sermon is doubtless as true (and as false) as when the originating preacher first said it.... Any decent public reader could do as much: it would be necessary only to supply the manuscript."[18]

Churches going this route could hire a "directional leader" to guide the church, removing the need for a preacher. Preachers could be making decisions today that result in their demise a few decades from now. So you think this could never happen? It already is happening. Heartland Community Church in Rockford, Illinois, currently relies on a videotape library of sermons. The church has no preaching pastor on its staff. The all-important measure of growth has occurred too. The church has grown from one hundred to three thousand in six years. Mark Bankord, who leads the church, prefers the title of the church's "directional leader." [19] If McChurching continues, this could be the wave of the future.

From a business standpoint, instead of hiring a preacher, why not hire a good writer and have that person write sermons for an actor. The writer will obviously do a better job than most preachers with content, and the actor will do a better job with delivery. This accomplishes the goal of predictability as we know we will experience a good sermon every week. It also accomplishes our goal of efficiency because we can pay the writer per sermon and the actor for a one-day performance and come out spending less money than by paying a full-time preacher. Churches employing writers is also already happening, and in some cases the writers are not believers. Haddon Robinson's daughter, "who frequently travels in her job, recently told [Robinson] about an experience she had when she struck up a conversation with a man on a recent flight who wrote sermons for pastors for an annual $500 subscription cost. 'As she talked further with this man, she quickly discovered that he wasn't a Christian,' Robinson said. 'She asked him how he could do sermons if he wasn't a Christian, to which he easily replied that he didn't have to study the Bible to put good thoughts together.'"[20]

We hope efficiency never becomes the standard for preaching, but from a purely business perspective, it could be just around the corner. If improved quality, better control, and more predictability are desired, this new method meets the criteria. The McChurching of America could result in preacherless churches and sermons written by people who do not believe in Christianity. This is but one reason we must begin to abandon McChurching.

Problem Number 2: No More Wrestling with Scripture

Consumerism among ministers also deprives the minister of struggling with the text of Scripture. Through struggling with the text, ministers grow spiritually and develop reliance upon the Holy Spirit for illumination. When preachers download sermons, they instead develop a reliance upon the Internet and begin to appreciate other gifted communicators over God's Word. D. A. Carson expressed it well.

> I am not referring to the almost inevitable borrowings of a person who reads a great deal, still less to the acknowledged borrowings of an honest worker, but to the wholesale reproducing of another's work as if it were your own. My concern here, however, is not so much with the immorality of such conduct as with the desperately tragic way in which it reduces preaching and the preacher, and finally robs the congregation.... But here there is no honest wrestling with the text, no unambiguous play of biblical truth on human personality, no burden from the Lord beyond mere play-acting, no honest interaction with and reflection on the words of God such that the preacher himself is increasingly conformed to the likeness of Christ.[21]

With the pastors relying more on the power of the Internet than the illumination of the Holy Spirit, one must wonder what the real message being communicated to the congregation is? Do we rely on God, or do we rely on technology?

Problem Number 3: A Loss of Credibility Damages Your Ability to Present the Gospel

Another major problem of this form of consumption comes when the sermon is regurgitated without being processed through the personal gifts of the preacher. Some would call this plagiarism, and, as you have seen, others call it effectiveness. All would agree that to do this too often for too long and of the same preacher is a problem. For example, when a member discovered that Rev. Alvin O'Neal Jackson, characterized as a "shining star" of his denomination, had preached the sermons of Rev. Thomas K. Tewell a problem arose. While some favor preaching others' sermons, no one has condoned Jackson's actions. He "even used Mr. Tewell's talks in a 12-week series he preached that was recorded and sold for $50."[22]

In addition, a denominational magazine, *Disciples World,* "discovered that one of Mr. Jackson's messages that had been published … had borrowed large sections from a 1982 book by another minister."[23] This too posed a problem. Jackson received credit in publications for words and thoughts that he had not personalized, and the fact that Jackson profited from Tewell's sermons resulted in his eventual resignation from the church.

If one cannot profit from or receive credit for another's work without personalizing it, then how can a person preach a sermon taken in majority from someone else? We do not believe a preacher should plagiarize in the pulpit. He risks losing credibility, which must be maintained when the gospel of Jesus Christ is at stake. Even if the sermons preached lack eloquence or great wisdom or creativity, the Holy Spirit uses "the foolishness of the message preached" to call people to salvation (see 1 Cor. 1:21). The temporal concerns of people just mentioned result from a desire for the preacher to be praised and from the consumerism of the congregations. The preacher must recognize that the gospel is "the power of God for salvation to everyone who believes" and that it is God's Word that will not return empty (see Rom. 1:16 and Isa. 55:11).

Another more prevalent problem is known as "ministerially speaking." Whether it is an exaggerated story or reporting of over-inflated church roles, anything beyond the truth jeopardizes the integrity of the preacher. Suppose you applied for a loan from the bank. The lender asks you how much money you make in a year. You tell the lender that you make two thousand dollars a week, knowing that your weekly paycheck never shows more than eight hundred dollars. When discovering this fact, the lender would ask you why you lied to him. What the banker wants is *real* numbers, not inflated numbers stating what the person thinks he should make or even what he may have made in the past. The bank needs the numbers that are current.

When we say we have two thousand members and never see more than eight hundred at one time, are we not guilty of a similar stretching of the truth? We are not saying that ministers intentionally lie when presenting inflated church roles, but we do not believe it is healthy for a church to claim as members those individuals who rarely ever enter the doors of the church. In addition to being inflated, it undermines the importance of membership and the cost of belonging to a Christian church. Ministerially speaking should not refer to exaggeration and a lack of accuracy, which may undermine our presentation of "the way, the truth, and the life."

Problem Number 4: Sermons of Milk and No Meat

Perhaps the greatest battle during the modern age surrounds the content of preaching. Congregations, and to a large degree pulpit committees, do not understand what type of preaching they need. Most of the general rules for popular preachers include a vibrant personality, good jokes, and personal illustrations; however, the content needed includes solid explanation of the text. The major difference is whether the preacher brings an idea to the text looking for support or comes to the text looking to reveal God's truth. Although this may be oversimplified, a text-driven preacher will allow God's Word to speak for itself. This type of preaching is what the congregation needs whether it desires it or not. This preaching may or may not result in increased numbers, but it certainly should result in spiritual growth and the gospel being presented.

The scriptural foundation for text-driven preaching flows logically from 2 Timothy 3:16—4:2. This portion of Scripture does cross a natural paragraph division, which has been divided as a new chapter. However, chapter 4 provides the application of the theological doctrine presented in 2 Timothy 3:16—4:2. Let us look at the text, and then we will explore the meaning:

All Scripture is inspired by God and profitable
for teaching, for reproof, for correction, for training in righteousness; so that the man of God

> may be adequate, equipped for every good
> work. I solemnly charge you in the presence
> of God and of Christ Jesus, who is to judge
> the living and the dead, and by His appearing
> and His kingdom: preach the word; be ready
> in season and out of season; reprove, rebuke,
> exhort, with great patience and instruction.

Without going into a detailed exegetical study, let's draw some implications that naturally link these verses together. Second Timothy 3:16 is the verse used to establish the authority of Scripture. Scripture is God breathed. Since God cannot lie and Scripture is God's Word to us, then Scripture can be trusted fully.

For our purposes is it important to notice what this verse says after that point: "for teaching, for reproof, for correction, for training in righteousness." After Paul has established the principle of the inerrancy of Scripture and that Scripture may be used for these reasons in preparing believers for every good work, he then solemnly charges Timothy to "preach the word." But notice what comes after "preach the word"—reprove, rebuke, exhort, and instruct. The end of 2 Timothy 4:2 should immediately bring to mind the words of 2 Timothy 3:16 as the application of the theological truth.

Let me explain it a different way. When you present a theological truth as a preacher, then most texts provide clues on the proper application to the listener's life. For example if the theological truth is that of salvation by grace through faith, the application is that the listener should place faith and trust in Jesus Christ to be saved. If the theological truth is to be holy as God is holy, the application is to avoid sinning and live a life consecrated to God, and specific examples may be given. Here Paul gives a theological truth: "Scripture is God breathed and profitable for teaching, for reproof, for correction, and for training in righteousness." The application of that truth is to "preach the word; be ready in season and out of season; reprove, rebuke, exhort ... and instruction."

Thus, text-driven preaching should be linked to the authority of Scripture. If you believe that God's Word is our final authority and sufficient to equip us for every good work, then what more do you have to add to it that God has not said? Do you believe that you can say it better than God? Do you not believe that God's Word is sufficient? Preaching that focuses on topics that the preacher brings to the Bible, perceived needs of the listener, or a preconceived notion that a preacher attempts to find a verse to support indicates that the preacher in practice does not believe God's Word is sufficient. In addition, it does not take seriously the fact that only "God's Word will not return void." John MacArthur has gone even further than we have by giving fifteen consequences of what he calls "Plexiglas Preaching."[24]

Some have made the objection that text-driven preaching is boring and that it does not always clearly apply to the listener. This objection is not with the method but with the preacher. No preacher of the gospel should be boring, nor should the preacher of the gospel fail to apply the text to the lives of the listeners. These claims throw the baby out with the bathwater. Proper text-driven preaching demands that the preacher communicates, engages, and shows Scripture's application to the listener. Thus, such claims find no merit against the proper method of preaching, however valid they may be against certain individual preachers. In fact, the objection itself indicates that the entertainment-driven consumer mentality has pervaded our expectation.

If text-driven preaching is the proper methodology, then the content should come from elaborating on a given passage of Scripture. The proper method does not mean coming to the text with an idea and then looking for support.[25] It means going to the text with a blank slate and learning what the text says, looking at the structure of the text, then expounding or explaining from the pulpit what the text says to the listeners. This also means preaching the whole counsel of God—the parts that are popular and the parts that are not popular. It means preaching on controversial issues, speaking prophetically to culture, encouraging the saint, challenging the sinner, and, most of all, glorifying God.

The preacher must ensure that he never compromises content for creativity. While nothing is wrong with using creative illustrations that fit the sermon, and even the use of video clips that enhance without overshadowing the message or sidetracking the congregation, the preacher must make sure the explanation of the text drives the sermon. Once a preacher begins sculpting a sermon around the illustration or video clip, then entertainment has taken an improper role in sermon preparation. The text itself must maintain priority. The tendency in ministry will be to emulate the more creative communicators, but the mandate for ministry is to preach the Word. No minister fails who faithfully explains the text of Scripture. He is at that moment God's messenger, and God maintains the responsibility for changing the lives of the hearers.

Consuming the Goods

The ultimate consumer who takes in products without thought of long-term consequences chooses the milkshake over something healthy every time. Dessert simply tastes better than the main course. That is why your mother always made you eat the meal before the reward—dessert. Today we have a society filled with consumers, which has resulted in congregations filled with consumers. Society has so infiltrated the church in this area that many do not notice it. Preachers consume sermons and then feed the consumer mentality of congregations through entertainment-based sermons and style options with video venues. The congregants wake up one day wondering "where's the beef?" in the messages, but by then they are so accustomed to the norm that they do not know how to change.

The pastor of the small local church winds up being the real loser in all of this. The rural-church, one-staff-member pastor finds himself involved in a high-tech war that he has not been prepared to fight. He knows little of video technology, and while struggling to grow, he finds few friends among the pastors of other congregations. Just when that small church comes close to breaking through a barrier so another staff member can be hired, a few more church members leave to enjoy the plethora of offerings at another church nearby.

Once again, too far away to think about supporting another staff member, the faithful servant feels betrayed by the consumer-feeding machine down the road that bears the name "church." Somehow it doesn't seem fair that he struggles to survive while preaching the Word as they sip coffee and watch high-definition television. So the rural country church finally gives in and becomes another site for the innovative church. The pastor becomes the campus pastor and before long is replaced by a new campus pastor who better understands the vision and identity of the main campus. Consumerism has won again, and a new congregation of consumers remains disconnected from each other but satisfied for the moment. The rural, now unemployed, pastor wonders if this is what Jesus meant when He said that the second commandment is love your neighbor as yourself (see Matt. 22:39). We have to stop and ask ourselves, "What are we doing?" Are we feeding the machine that may just undo the fabric of the church itself?

DRIVE THRU ⬆

I'll Take That to Go

- ▢ Learning from other preachers is encouraged, but the wholesale reproduction of another preacher's sermon is nothing more than intellectual
  plagiarism.

- ▢ Secular society has begun to take notice of "sermon stealing." Religious
  leaders need to begin addressing the issue before we harm our public
  witness.

- ▢ L. R. Scarborough said, "A head-liner preacher will sooner or later be a
  dead-liner preacher.... It thrives on excitement and demands so much
  more each time that the preacher cannot meet the demand and soon
  he fails."

- ▢ Some churches have abandoned preachers altogether, using various
  videotapes with a "directional leader."

- ▢ Text-driven preaching delivers the message of God's text to the listener
  and not the message of the church's preacher to the listener.

Health Inspector

- ▢ How do you balance your consumption of external resources (electronic
  material, commentaries, or other sermons) with your own studying, praying, and struggling through the text when preparing your messages?

- How much can you borrow from another preacher before the sermon is his instead of yours?

- When you stand behind the pulpit, would you prefer people to say "What a great preacher!" or "The preacher wasn't that great, but the Lord really spoke to me through the message"?

- Would you employ a nonbeliever's secular writing if people would consider you a better preacher because of it? Why or why not? What makes the content of your messages specifically Christian or specifically scriptural?

- How do you ensure your sermon presents the main point of the passage instead of presenting the point you want to make? How do you keep from using only a portion of the Scripture passage as support instead of struggling with the whole context of the passage?

CHAPTER SEVEN

Happy Meals for All?:
Theotainment in the Church

It was the summer of 1979. The McDonald's Corporation decided to try something new, so they created the Happy Meal. The top executives thought that the box would be what drew the kids to the meal, so they designed the first one in the shape of a circus train car.[1] However, they soon learned that kids tossed the boxes in the trash and kept the toy. "It's always been all about the toy," says Laura Dihel, a spokeswoman for McDonald's.[2] The toy drew the kids to McDonald's, which increased sales and pleased everyone.

McDonald's creatively made agreements with various groups, including Disney, My Little Pony, and any number of movie studios to offer toys of various kinds in the Happy Meals. Perhaps nothing has been as successful as the offering of a Beanie Baby in the fall of 1997. One article states:

> Actually, it was the doll tucked inside called a
> Teeny Beanie Baby that fueled the madness.
> The larger Beanie Baby plush toys already had
> stormed the market. Across the country, patrons
> lined up in the predawn hours before McDon-
> ald's opened to snag as many Happy Meals
> as possible just for the "babies." Sometimes,
> the food, untouched, was ditched in the near-
> est trash can. Before long, restaurants began
> posting limits of 10 Happy Meals per customer.[3]

Can you imagine a store limiting its sales of Happy Meals to ten per customer? At that point the toy had eclipsed the food, and for the sake of the business, the corporate office decided that action had to be taken in order to have food available for those who came to McDonald's for that purpose. Even the Happy Meal can go too far in creating sales. When the toy offered eclipses the food provided, a problem exists.

Many churches today have a similar issue. Just imagine with me the scene at one prominent church in America. The stage goes black. The audience leans forward in anticipation. Offstage, an engine begins to rev loudly. The beauty of the well-tuned Italian exhaust is missed by most of the congregation until the headlamps of a $150,000 Ferrari illuminate the now smoke-filled stage. Carefully, the car navigates onto the platform. The pastor jumps out onto the now fully lit stage and starts lauding the purposeful design and beauty of the car. The eyes of every boy stare at the exquisite curves and shiny rims of this work of art. The speaker begins to speak, but the audience gives little notice to the words coming from his mouth. It's more about the car than about the content.

Eventually the pastor stops commenting on the car and gets to the message, but the car remains onstage. After the service, you hear person after person commenting on the beauty of the car and the creativity of the speaker. We wonder how many heard the content of the message.

Just as the toy in the Happy Meal eclipses the sale of food, some creative sermon illustrations eclipse the content of the message. When a person's focus continues along the line of the illustration, the video, or in this case a Ferrari, then you may have moved into theotainment rather than preaching. Over-the-top illustrations or entertainment-driven communication encourages the consumer-based mentality among congregations and very often takes precedence over the gospel itself.

Illustrations and creativity certainly have a proper place in the preaching of the gospel. Jesus used illustrations or parables. The illustration can be the hammer that drives home the point. A misplaced illustration for the sake of amusement can be the sledgehammer that destroys the building blocks of content. The central point of the message must come first—the biblical truth is primary. Additionally, if a speaker spends more time developing an illustration than researching the content of a passage, then the speaker has placed the cart before the horse. The congregation rarely comments on the problem and likely compliments the creativity, not recognizing that the toy has eclipsed the main reason for being there. Rest assured that such entertaining communication will draw lines of consumers, just as the tiny Beanie Babies did.

Theotainment and the Church

The Happy Meals of McDonald's or Disneyfication does have its limits. Standing in an interminable line at a Disney ride tends to lead to wandering eyes. You see a child lose her ice cream over at the ice-cream stand, or you notice that one area of the park that seems to have escaped the ubiquitous trash sweeper. You begin to realize that some of the paid cast members don't care too much about the alternate reality you are experiencing. Despite all the charm and delight, at some point, even the Magic Kingdom loses its magic.

Back in 1985, Neil Postman suggested that Americans were amusing themselves to death.[4] Arguing that television produced a shift in dialogue that reorganized what was important to people, Postman believed that incoherence would ultimately be the result of such progress. People, events, and even religion would lose their context in a society that provided no coherent place for the exchange of ideas. According to Postman, people would begin inventing contexts, or pseudocontexts, so that the useless, random information they consumed would have meaning. Postman warned that as this begins to happen, these pseudocontexts, which seemingly give structure to otherwise "fragmented and irrelevant information," would not provide a call to action, societal change, or even aid in the process of dealing with societal problems. Instead, the pseudocontext, according to Postman, has only one purpose: to amuse.[5]

Churches, once a niche market with strong denominational "brand identity," presented the good news from within the boundaries of their ecclesiological systems. While evangelicalism provided some level of interaction between these churches, especially in relationship to evangelism, each denomination had its own strong cultural markers.

Today, recognizing the void people face in relation to life and its fragmentation in American culture, churches have been all too happy to interject their own unique brands of religious expression. In the attempt to share the Jesus of the gospel, however, churches can unintentionally find themselves capitulating to the culture in order to draw a crowd. They become the purveyors of religious amusement—theotainment.

Theotainment is an attempt to utilize entertainment to fill the spiritual needs of the church attendees. This reveals itself on many levels, from musical performance to the content of messages, which frequently contain nothing unique from self-help gurus like Tony Robbins. In the end, the people attending walk away reflecting on a spiritual experience and feeling good about themselves and their life circumstances, but missing the hard teachings of the Word.

Historically, this is nothing new. For the last two hundred years, evangelicals have been the best at capturing cultural trends and readapting them for their own purposes. Historian Nathan Hatch has argued that the process of the democratization of American religion depended upon individual pastors or leaders who were able to capture the hearts and minds of the audience.[6] Nineteenth-century itinerates, like Lorenzo Dow, quickly realized that pairing emotive music to their theatrical-style presentations of the gospel would engender greater results numerically.

D. L. Moody and Ira Sankey perhaps captured this *modus operandi* most effectively on both sides of the Atlantic, leading scores to walk the so-called Sawdust Trail to salvation. Billy Sunday, former baseball player turned evangelist, would frequently run onto the stage and then slide into the pulpit as if he were stretching for home plate. Jumping up from the ground and mimicking the umpire, Sunday would waive his arms and yell, "SAFE!" at the top of his lungs. His theatrics captivated his audience and led to scores of conversions of those who wanted to be "safe" for all of eternity.

A primary attraction at any McChurch in America is the ability of the pastorpreneur to mix the right level of entertainment with content transmission.[7] Boring equals death in the terms of a church. The more a church can reinvent itself in successive, more dynamic versions, the more it will grow. Many times rapid adjustments to keep in tune with the culture could be accomplished only by itinerate evangelists. Pastors and church leaders frequently look to these evangelists as the benchmark for success.

Think of your experiences at a Billy Graham event. John Mark served with a group that headed up the decision counselors for the 1998 Indianapolis crusade. Why did so many people turn out to hear Billy Graham? Was it the themed music nights that featured everything from bluegrass to rock and roll? Just like the revivalists at the turn of the twentieth century, the Billy Graham team knew how to capture the attention of a city through mass marketing, entertaining musical groups, and the charisma of Billy Graham himself. A simple observation of today's most successful congregations reveals that they are typically those that capture the heart of what one would expect at a Billy Graham crusade and package it for a more permanent locale.[8]

The people want to be entertained, so give them what they want.

Must a church entertain, however? Think of countless children's ministries across the United States. Destined to be the future leaders of the church, what has been the steady diet of many of these young adults? Entertainment. Most children's Sunday schools quit reading and studying the Bible long ago. Instead, children view cartoon adaptations of the text along with numerous activities that keep them entertained while Mom and Dad worship without distraction. Moving to youth groups, many of these same kids rely on emotional experiences, graphical images, game times, and vacuous messages. The churches that have the largest population of students are frequently those that provide the best entertainment for the kids. In many towns, the religiously oriented youth, savvy shoppers that they are, simply attend the church that has the greatest concentration of entertaining events.

Assuming these young adults stay in church (which is the last thing we should assume given the statistics), what do we assume their expectations for church services will be? Society has trained them to be careful consumers, with an uncanny ability to ferret out what best suits their personal desires. Christianity, for many in American culture, is simply a selection on the Buffet of Religion. If they buy into Christianity through entertainment, the show must go on to keep them engaged. Thanks to the law of diminishing returns, that same show must continue to attract their attention with newer or greater things, or else these shoppers will find another, more interesting show down the road, which may or may not be another church.

Unfortunately this show also tends toward the discount purveyors of the product. Consumer culture elevates consumer desires to near-deified status. Trying to hook the consumer with marketing, many brands attract customers by offering steep discounts on their product. Unfortunately, many churches across America are attracting ever-greater numbers into their congregation not only through their ability to amuse and entertain but also by their insistence that consumers of their goods do not have to do anything. The pastors and staff control almost all aspects of the daily needs of the congregation, leaving little for the average person to do but attend.

Life in the Religious Economy

Christian megachurches are fast becoming the darlings of sociological research when it comes to analyzing how one packages the perfect product (one that is available 24/7/365 and aids in most everything) and "pitches" it to the masses. In *Shopping for God*, James Twitchell discusses our need for choice: "AT&T offering 'the right choice'; Wendy's, 'there is no better choice'; Pepsi, 'the choice of a new generation'; Coke, 'the real choice'; and Taster's Choice Coffee is 'the choice for taste.'"[9] Twitchell points to the Harvard study on Willow Creek, commenting that "all in all, concluded the Harvard study, Willow Creek is a tribute to 'knowing your customers and meeting their needs.'"[10] As American pastorpreneurs jump into the "scramble economy," Twitchell finds it more than ironic that "some Christian denominations don't care for the Darwinian model when applied to biology or social engineering, yet they themselves have to hustle, innovate, adapt, mutate, grow new appendages, or become the lunch of those who do."[11] As evangelicals, we understand the centrality of the gospel and the importance of communicating that message, but are we missing the point in communicating it?

In one of the most telling books released recently, *Reveal: Where Are You?*, Greg Hawkins and Cally Parkinson analyzed Willow Creek and other leading churches to determine the effectiveness of the

theories many of the megas base their churches upon.[12] Many of
them discovered that where they had been placing their emphases
did not, in fact, net them the best results. Instead, the slow process
of training and discipling adult followers always garnered more effective long-term results in every case. This has led to a new vision for
how ministry is being conducted at Willow Creek and even led to
questioning of the homogenous growth principle. These are interesting days indeed.

Churches feel the pressure, real or imagined, to keep up. Capitulating to the trends of the day, the churches focus on making attendees
feel good about themselves, their experience, and life in general. Basing
success on the number of attendees, churches lose sight of Jesus' radical claims against the culture of His day as well as our own. Church
consumers become like kids in search of the Happy Meal that has
the best movie or TV tie-in. The food doesn't matter as long as the
prize inside is good. And there is never a warning on the box that
regular consumption can be hazardous to your health. To cite Neil
Postman again: "I believe I am not mistaken in saying that Christianity
is a demanding and serious religion. When it is delivered as easy and
amusing, it is another kind of religion altogether."[13]

Congregation as Consumer

Consumerism has recently been the subject of a full edition of *Leadership Journal*. Skye Jethani argued that consumerism actually seeks
to replace religion. "Ads became the prophets of capitalism—turning
the hearts of the people toward the goods they didn't know they
needed."[14] And what's worse is that consumerism is winning. "Obesity, sexual promiscuity, and skyrocketing credit card debt are just a

few signs."[15] Whether consumerism will replace religion is beyond the scope of this discussion, but no one would argue that consumerism has not affected religion.

Congregations demonstrate a consumer mentality in many ways, one of which is the preferred style of sermon delivery. While one would assume that all people prefer to hear the preacher live and in person, some, especially younger members of the congregation, may prefer to watch in the video venue. "Walter Jones, a member of New Life Christian Church in Centerville, Virginia, says that his 15-year old son prefers watching the sermon on video. He says that his teenager would not attend service at all if it were not for the televised sermons."[16]

Jones goes on to explain, "Most people would say, 'Well, that's crazy. Why would you want something on a screen when you can see someone live?' But my son plays a lot of video games, he goes online, he does his schoolwork on the computer, so he's used to it. It's very relaxing for him."[17] With a new generation so accustomed to watching screens, the preacher on a screen seems normal. From watching our GPS screens in the car to our DVD players at home and our laptop screens at work, adding the screen to the worship house seems natural for the next generation. In fact, it's the interaction with the live person that seems abnormal.

Other members of the congregation prefer to interact with a live person. One article addresses it as follows:

Beth Cygon, 39, a member of New Life Church, says that she just cannot get used to her church's

> new video café room. "I love the direct connection
> with the person up front," she said. "As a minis-
> ter you might be moved to speak about a certain
> thing. You can cue off how a crowd is reacting
> and change the direction of what you are doing.
> That's ... impossible with a video service."[18]

While this may make up the majority preference of the attendees at churches, that could be changing.

Others may choose not to go to a church at all. George Barna
discusses this phenomena in his book *Revolution*. [19] A possible
wave of the future could be that individuals abandon the church
for a more personal religion. Instead of an institutional church, these
people create their own potpourri of religious expression. This
concept known as customization can be seen in the iPod. "No
longer is a listener required to buy an entire CD to enjoy just
one song."[20] Consumers may customize their choices in the form
of TV sermons, combined with visiting a virtual church through
the Internet or listening to sermons on podcast while fishing and
absorbing the beauty of God's creation. Whatever the spiritual
influence, with so many products being offered, the true consumer
picks and chooses which product fits his or her given needs during
a given moment. With a loss of commitment and no long-term
dedication to any institution, the true end of consumer-driven
religion is an individual pick-and- choose religion that finds no
ties binding one to messy relationships and institutions.

Another potential problem developing over style comes in
the facilities, environment, or surroundings. For those who accept

watching a video screen, a plethora of personal choices may exist. "At one church, upon arriving each family member can choose the worship setting that fits their personal desire. Simultaneously, grandma can sing hymns in the traditional service, mom and dad can enjoy coffee and bagels in the worship café, and the teenagers can lose their hearing in the rock venue."[21] "While the head pastor preaches live in a more traditional service in another room, people in the 'video café' see only his talking head on a screen."[22]

At North Coast Church, you can choose from "five different venues for worship. The church calls its main sanctuary setting 'North Coast Live.' Video Cafe was the first alternative venue established in 1998."[23] In this setting you can sit in patio chairs while enjoying danishes and Starbucks coffee. Another service is called "Traditions." "It's described as an 'intimate and nostalgic worship experience led from a baby grand piano—a mix of classic hymns, old favorites and contemporary worship choruses.'"[24] Perhaps the most creative version called The Edge "resembles a nightclub, with a high-energy band and big subwoofers."[25]

This unique religious-business model offers "a collection of smaller worship rooms connected to a larger congregation [which] provides the best of both worlds—economies of scale for a large organization and the intimacy of smaller worship circles."[26] Others have responded to such offerings by saying, "Our concern becomes not whether people are growing but whether they are satisfied. An unhappy member, like an unhappy customer, will find satisfaction elsewhere."[27]

The basic reasoning behind the move reveals the consumer mentality of our culture. "Just as a retail store wouldn't dream of offering only one style of clothing or shoes, more large churches are concluding that a single type of worship service is inadequate to meet the needs of the entire congregation. This is why many churches today hold 'contemporary' services simultaneously with traditional services."[28]

While this mentality produces success (if measuring by numbers), the model feeds the consumer mentality. North Coast Church has more than six thousand attendees with rooms that hold no more than six hundred. By most standards, this model has achieved success, but by offering additional styles or products with the same video message, individualism is encouraged, and consumerism is reinforced. Instead of learning to care for the elderly or widows, to pray for those not like yourself, you become a religious consumer simply seeking to have it your way. One has to stop and ask what this practice will do to the next generation of congregants.

This problem also exists in women's ministry groups where churches choose to watch a video series rather than have someone a little less entertaining speak and bring the message. Even in these venues, the replacement of speakers by video inhibits the development of future leaders. Video presentations rob the women of interaction and specific application.

Only the Happy (Good) News, Please

We should not be surprised that congregations all across America order spiritual Happy Meals every Sunday. Scripture tells us in 2 Timothy 4:3–4 (NKJV), "For the time will come when they will not endure sound doctrine, but according to their own desires, because they have itching ears, they will heap up for themselves teachers; and they will turn their ears away from the truth, and be turned aside to fables." By this we do not mean to imply that all congregations desire to find those who will tickle their ears, but some certainly do. Humans would rather avoid their sinfulness than confront it. We do not like facing the truth. We find it much easier to ignore sinful desires and continue living in blissful ignorance.

Congregations seeking Happy Meals will not tolerate difficult messages and do not want to hear the full gospel. One of the largest churches in America does a great job of preaching "happy news." The congregants are encouraged to live their best life now and taught how to do that each and every week. The speaker teaches mostly biblical principles, and the congregation always leaves feeling uplifted. From a marketing standpoint, this could be considered the pinnacle of perfection.

The questions arise not from what the speaker says as much as what the speaker doesn't say. With certain facts rarely ever mentioned at all, one wonders if the full gospel of Jesus Christ is being presented. Just what is being left out, and do the missing parts affect our eternal destiny?

Rarely do we hear speakers say that following Christ may result in losing your life. In fact, this seems contrary to the positive message conveyed in living your best life on this earth. Should living your best life now be applied to the disciples, then they failed miserably. All of the disciples but one died a martyr's death for the cause of Christ. The only disciple to live a full life and die of "natural causes" was John, and he died in exile on the island of Patmos. However, the positive message draws huge crowds. Does it communicate the true gospel or only a spiritual genie able to take care of our problems? The "happy news" does not fit with Matthew 10:38–39 (NKJV); "And he who does not take his cross and follow after Me is not worthy of Me. He who finds his life will lose it, and he who loses his life for My sake will find it."

The "happy news" does not communicate that a Christian's reward is in heaven. The message focuses on instant gratification and not eternal perspective. The congregation wants rewards in this life and immediate benefit. However, the New Testament states in Matthew 6:19–21 (NKJV), "Do not lay up for yourselves treasures on earth, where moth and rust destroy and where thieves break in and steal; but lay up for yourselves treasures in heaven, where neither moth nor rust destroys and where thieves do not break in and steal. For where your treasure is, there your heart will be also."

Although this will be discussed in more detail later, one final problem comes with a lack of preparation for suffering. The "happy news" presented at some consumer-driven churches appears to be a magic wand, a talisman, or an additional feature that simply makes living the current life better. For some, God becomes a fairy godmother whom they call upon whenever something new is needed. For others, the gift of God appears to be a bonus offer of eternal fire insurance. So while experiencing all that the world has to offer, they simply add on this "God thing" to make their experience even better. For others the gospel is like an extra feature on a new car. Although there is nothing wrong with this life and they see no problem that needs fixing, God can enrich the experience and be there just in case He is needed.

"Happy news" presents half-truths and not the full story. When living the Christian life becomes tough, the consumer abandons "the way" because they did not sign up for troubles, only for rewards. However, the New Testament tells believers to expect trouble and never promises a life free of tribulation. John 16:33 (NKJV) says, "These things I have spoken to you, that in Me you may have peace. In the world you will have tribulation; but be of good cheer, I have overcome the world."

In order to understand the good news, one must understand the bad news. The bad news is that we have all sinned. We have broken God's law, and now we owe a debt that we cannot pay. If left to our own means, we deserve death, hell, and eternal punishment. Yet God loved us so much that while we were yet sinners, Christ died for us. We must understand our current state of depravity to understand the good news found in the substitutionary death of Jesus Christ.

Our supreme example of this principle is Jesus Christ. Jesus knew nothing of consumerism and materialism on this earth. The Creator of the universe came to earth, where He was persecuted, ridiculed, and crucified. The Creator came to the creature who treated Him with distain, and yet He prayed, "Father, forgive them." Can we really expect any better than what our Master had on this earth? Our Lord's words are recorded in Luke 9:58 (NKJV): "And Jesus said to him, 'Foxes have holes and birds of the air have nests, but the Son of Man has nowhere to lay His head.'" Should we expect our best life now, when Jesus did not have a place to lay His head and experienced great persecution on this earth?

Congregational Stockholders

Perhaps the most destructive way the congregation acts as a consumer comes from the pressure for growth on the pastor. Many pastors of small churches do everything they possibly can to help those churches grow. Despite pastors best efforts, the churches do not seem to grow. As if the pastor does not feel enough pressure from other successful pastors, friends who compare numbers, the local association or state conventions comparing numbers, and every preaching conference highlighting growing churches, the pastor's own congregation believes that growth represents God's blessing and that if the congregation doesn't grow, then the pastor must be doing something wrong. While most healthy churches do grow at a reasonable rate, most congregations expect unreasonable growth without doing their part to make such growth occur.

Perhaps the best comparison for this form of consumer mentality equates to that of a stockholder in a publicly traded company. While the stockholders spend no personal time or energy working for the company, they expect a return on their investment of money. The expected return in stocks is increased revenue. In the spiritual world, the expected return is increased membership and increased income. This expectation creates unnecessary pressure upon the preacher and fosters a consumer-driven mentality in which the preacher must satisfy customers and keep the stockholders off his back.

If we could find a way to eliminate this one form of consumerism, our churches and preachers would become instantly healthier. If congregants measured pastoral success by a combination of the spiritual walk of the minister, the spiritual growth of congregants, the number of ministers called out from under his leadership, and the number of churches planted, then pastors in various areas could all feel successful rather than having to endure the pressure of continually growing numbers.

Moving to the Grown-ups' Table

To some degree church leaders are tied to congregations. After all, who would you preach to if no one showed up to hear you? The pressure quickly mounts to generate satisfied customers and keep the masses happy. As great as the pressure from the consumer-driven congregations might be, the preacher of the gospel must remember that he serves an audience of One. That "One" is the Holy One. Imagine the pressure Noah faced when building a boat on dry land. Imagine the pressure Moses faced as he confronted the rebellious Israelites about idolatry. Imagine the pressure the Old Testament prophets felt while preaching negative messages of impending doom among hostile crowds. Yet these men were God's messengers. They served no man, and their reward is eternal. Congregational consumerism is not right, and the fully devoted followers of Christ must never give in to it. The only "Happy Meal" the Christian is ever promised comes with the words of Christ when He says, "Well done, My good and faithful servant." Remember this, and your reward will be great.

DRIVE THRU ⬆

I'll Take That to Go

- Videos, illustrations, and even application can be so creative that they distract from rather than reinforce the message of the text.

- In an attempt at sharing the Jesus of the gospel, churches can unintentionally find themselves the purveyors of religious amusement—theotainment.

- Through various video venues, churches can reinforce the consumer mentality among the attendees by offering choices that appeal to personal preferences.

- If living our best life on earth is the standard, then Jesus and the disciples failed miserably. This should cause us to prepare for tribulation while on earth.

- Pressure, real or imagined, to increase numbers or giving can create challenges for the leaders of the church.

Health Inspector

- How do you distinguish between creativity in your ministry and providing entertainment?

- What is it your listener focuses on after hearing the message? The text, the illustrations, the presentation, etc. . . .

- If you trained your church leaders to be "consumer free," what would the structure of your church look like? How many of your existing programs would remain?

▣ In what ways are you tempted to help your congregation feel "happy" about life? Do you avoid any passages of Scripture because a large giver or prominent person might be offended?

▣ Does watching a video of a gifted speaker inhibit the development of members to become speakers or teachers themselves? Why or why not?

▣ What compromises have you witnessed in your ministry or the ministries of others in order to simply increase numbers?

▣ How does your church develop disciples? How do you transition Christians from seeking a spiritual Happy Meal to "craving the meat of the Word"?

CHAPTER EIGHT

The Multisite Movement: Feeding Consumerism

"Don't you know that 90 percent of all church plants fail?"

Though I doubted his statistic, this was not a great way to start a conversation on why churches choose to go multisite over planting a church.

"Don't you think that some of the failures are the result of poor planning or ill-equipped church planters? Don't you think that someone you mentored and sponsored would have the ability to succeed?" I asked.

"The right person just is not present," he responded.

And with that, another of my friends embarked upon the multisite experiment.

The result of the multisite movement is a *campus* pastor who can teach and does so in small-group settings but not at corporate worship. One wonders why the campus pastor cannot preach to the crowd. In order for the campus pastor to fit the scriptural qualifications of a pastor or elder, 1 Timothy 3:2 says he must be "able to teach." If the campus pastor is able to teach, then why spend money piping in another preacher? The obvious answer comes from the fact that the campus pastor does not have the creative-speaking ability, the biblical knowledge, the charisma, or the sense of humor the preacher at the "founding" campus does.

Here are our problems with this line of logic: (1) This seems to overlook the sovereignty of God and the necessity of prayer and support in church plants. Because 90 percent of church plants don't work, we, the humans, have to fix the problem for God, the Creator. Many of those involved in this movement do not hold to a small view of God. Some even claim Reformed theology, and yet their ecclesiology becomes small and wrapped up in human action with little divine intervention. (2) This logic states that the lead pastor at the main church is so gifted that he cannot be replaced elsewhere. The entire concept of discipleship is replication. If Christians cannot replicate themselves, then the future is in trouble. If we multiply disciples through replication, then we have a larger impact.

Instead of gifted communicators at the main campus insisting upon being broadcast at the video venue, perhaps the main teacher should substitute others for himself. The principle to learn is that personality-based ministries have no place in God's church. We do not support poor teaching but rather supervised teaching that allows others' experience and trains both the teacher and the congregation that God's work is bigger than any one of us. A second idea would be to place one of those mentored teachers as a leader in the multisite location. This location would have the right in the constitution to separate from the original location upon congregational vote.

The insistence upon one person preaching through all video

venues comes across as emphasizing the ministry and gifting of one person over all others. We know many of these are great Bible teachers with great hearts, but this insistence leads us to believe that they think others cannot teach as well as they can and that God cannot work through lesser communicators. In addition, the message communicated to the staff or congregations is that only the most creative and polished humans can accomplish God's work.

Somehow this does not seem to fit with Jesus' selection of Peter as one of those who would proclaim the gospel or Moses, who complained that he did not speak well, to lead the children of Israel. In fact, our only hope for ministry is that God can in fact use the foolish of this world to confound the wise and hit straight licks with crooked sticks. Without intending to do so, the multisite movement promotes an air of elitism and discourages the common person from being bold for God. It also diminishes the gospel as the power of God. The men we know involved in this movement do not intend such a message, but they are unintentionally encouraging such perspectives.

If the most important credential for preaching and worshipping comes from creativity and entertainment, then perhaps America should rethink religion. All congregations would benefit from hearing the most creative or most knowledgeable communicator in America. For the sake of argument, let's say that the best preacher would be Jerry Vines (which happens to correspond to Thomas's view). Every church in America would hear Jerry Vines every Sunday. In addition, if you are only going to watch the best preacher on a screen, then why can you not watch him in the comfort of your home on television or on your computer? You can even pay your tithe through

PayPal or a Web site that takes credit cards, and you never have to leave the comfort of your home. *Koinonia* or fellowship, you scream, will be lost forever—but wait, many of us have better relationships with some of our "online friends" through instant messaging, text messaging, Facebook, and chat rooms than we do with some people who sit across from us every Sunday at church.

Perhaps one preacher will not do, but perhaps the ten most creative pastors could be selected so that we could choose between the most creative storyteller, the most creative in application, or the most creative in biblical exposition. The biggest payoff from all this is that we can spend our money sending missionaries abroad rather than on brick and mortar. No more air-conditioning bills, and the issue of space will never again cause problems. While we do not believe the evangelical church will reach this point, the next generation could take religion in America to this level. At this level the "assembly," or *ecclesia,* would be no more.

Some in the multisite movement appeal to Paul's letters and argue that he would have used video had it been an option. Perhaps he would have, but we question whether Paul would have placed himself as bishop over the many congregations he helped plant. For argument's sake, let's grant that Paul would have used video. Would Paul have told the church at Corinth "when you are assembled … deliver such a one to Satan" (1 Cor. 5:4–5)? Notice Paul told the congregation to "deliver such a one to Satan." He upheld the congregational responsibility even in the mentoring relationship.

If he had been able, Paul might have used the video venue to help deliver occasional messages and encouragement to congregations that he helped plant and then turned control over to the local congregation and the local pastor. According to the pattern in Scripture, it does not seem clear that Paul would have established nor intended to establish interconnected, multiple-location churches under the domination of a central congregation.

Paul wrote in Philippians 2:3–5, "Do nothing from selfishness or empty conceit, but with humility of mind regard one another as more important than yourselves; do not merely look out for your own personal interests, but also for the interests of others. Have this attitude in yourselves which was also in Christ Jesus." We do not see how the multisite movement can demonstrate this attitude on a corporate level or a personal one.

How can preachers argue that they are more gifted than others at teaching God's Word and still "esteem others better than themselves"? Churches cannot move into areas with the industrial machine and overrun small struggling churches and "look out not only for his own interests, but also the interests of others." Calvin Pearson says it well: "I must admit that too often, I step into the pulpit fully prepared with my words so that when I step out I will be fully affirmed by the words of others. Unfortunately, at that point, my motive is not love for God and others but love for myself."[1] The entire concept of not encouraging church plants because you will lose key givers is void of having "this mind … also in Christ Jesus," who gave up all the riches of heaven to come to earth with nothing.

We write these words with utmost respect for the many who disagree with our position, and we mean no disrespect to those great men; however, it is the case that great pastors and church leaders often find themselves surrounded with people who encourage the desire to expand the ministry, rather than those who would caution and disagree with the primary leader.

At the very least, we wish these words to be a heartfelt caution to the gifted leaders in our churches to:

1) Avoid feeding the consumer mentality of congregations looking to hear entertaining communicators over less entertaining yet equally accurate teachers.

2) Avoid listening to those who puff up your ego.

3) Avoid the tendency to use your personality to attract people to you rather than to point people to Jesus Christ.

4) Attempt to promote others and replicate yourself rather than continuously building ministries centered on you.

We hope these words come across as intended. We have a sincere desire to see healthy churches that reach our nation and the world for Jesus Christ. In order for this to happen, our gifted teachers and preachers must lead efforts to create more leaders and more teachers to help proclaim the gospel to the ends of the earth.

Planting Growing Churches

Dr. Gene Getz, church planter and pastor emeritus of Fellowship Bible North, now known as Chase Oaks Church, reflected on the issue of church planting and satellite campuses with us.[2] "When I was planting churches in the 1970s, satellite technology was not an option," Dr. Getz said. "We only thought in terms of starting self-contained churches and being decentralized."

Their strategy was simple: Each church should plant at least one other congregation during its life cycle. Out of the first church they started, a large number of elders came from a particular community.

"We saw this as God's leading for us to start a new congregation in that location," Dr. Getz said. "Those elders would start the new plant and eventually hire a pastor."

Fellowship Bible Church repeated this process multiple times. Some of the congregations stayed relatively small, but several of the church plants grew in excess of four thousand people. "If I wanted to count them all, we have over thirty thousand regular worshippers in locations started from our single church. But each of those churches are independent and free to reach the communities where they were planted." As many of these congregations grew, they also have started new church plants in other communities to continue reaching more people with the gospel.

Dr. Getz admits that one of the attractions of the satellite movement is the emphasis on polished teaching. "The key for any church is that the teaching of Scripture must be strong." When churches emphasize watered-down teaching in hopes of attracting seekers, that ministry suffers from a fatal flaw. "Weak teaching equals weak results. If a church believes it ought to move to a satellite format, it must hinge everything on strong biblical teaching. Teach the Word in depth and with quality, and unbelievers will still come to the gospel. But they will do so with understanding instead of responding to teaching that does not have depth."

Numbers-Driven Success

Another problem, not limited to, but troubling within the multisite methodology is the tendency to judge the success of the church by the number of members—the "calculability" factor we mentioned before. While it is true, at least in theory, that each number represents a life won for Christ, the problem comes when numbers mark success instead of changed lives. Numbers can result from transfer growth as documented by William Chadwick in *Stealing Sheep: The Church's Hidden Problems with Transfer Growth*. While discussing the church-growth movement, this book points out that the "American church had not increased in numbers during the decade of church growth."[3] While individual congregations may increase in numbers, this may not represent new people being added to God's kingdom.

Church-growth principles have encouraged the multisite movement because some churches have simply run out of space or reached that magical 80 percent rule—the rule that says once you hit 80 percent of your auditorium's capacity, then you must go to a second service or look for other options, which may include multisite methodology. In order to be a successful congregation, the church must reach more people—the congregation must expand. Sometimes building a larger building is not possible because of city restrictions or finances. Whatever the reasons, many churches are choosing the multisite option to increase numbers and continue growth, since growth equals success.

Because Chadwick demonstrates that numbers do not always represent changed lives, perhaps we should measure success based on how many churches a congregation can plant rather than people in a pew. Perhaps we can measure success based on how many missionaries and pastors a congregation sends out. Perhaps we can measure success based on the integrity of the membership, the practice of church discipline, and the preaching of the Word. When we pray that God moves mightily in our cities, are we okay if our church is not the one experiencing the growth during the mighty movement?

Imagine if Home Depot built a new store right next to an older Home Depot. The new store claims success because it has a great client base. Being the newer store with a larger building and better-lit parking lot provides enough advantage for this store to be the choice store. The old Home Depot slowly begins to dwindle, while the new store blossoms. Has the new store been successful? No! It has not brought new clients to Home Depot. It has not taken clients from a competitor. It has not encouraged more people to do home projects. The store has simply stolen members from an existing and similar store. The home company will not be pleased with the effects of the new store. Similarly, creating a more entertaining church to draw church members from less entertaining churches is not proper church growth but is unspiritual entertainment-driven member swiping.[4] If church growth comes from new believers, then praise the Lord; but if the growth comes from another existing church, then what good has been accomplished?

The Small-Church Pastor

If anyone needs encouragement, it is the small-church pastor. I (Thomas) am very proud of my roommate in seminary. Although we came to seminary with completely opposite characteristics, I have watched from afar as he has faithfully shepherded a small congregation in Florida. By all that I know, he has done an excellent job of preaching the Word and loving the people. He is the lone full-time staff member in his church and the only employee most of his church members have. He lives right next door to the church, and the last time we talked, he liked it that way. In my mind, no church could do better than to have someone so committed and loving as pastor.

In fact, when we reach heaven, some of these committed followers of Christ will receive a larger reward than more prominent members of our religious fraternities. I believe the faithful servants behind the scenes who never attempt to publicize themselves, who never receive human accolades, and who never gain a "following" may receive more rewards than the household names we would know.

The servants who serve some smaller congregations and do not have the large salaries will inherit great eternal reward. Those who live on a meager income in order to work for God's kingdom will inherit great eternal reward. Those who hear little praise from the mouths of people but consistently and faithfully preach the Word will inherit great eternal reward. Some Christian superstars have already received their reward, while the unknown soldier marches on for God's kingdom.

Yet some faithful soldiers feel as if they gained new enemies in the form of multisite movements from large congregations located far away. The gifted personality already serving with great reward and fruit comes to town in order to establish a new location with all the resources of the main campus backing it. Some of these pastors don't know what to do. They gave their lives in service to God's kingdom, while others came in and took over what they labored hard to build in the name of Christ.

Even Internet churches pull from members of smaller churches, harming their ability to reach their communities. Some members leave for a more entertaining style of worship or more creative communicator.[5] Before you think it can't happen, consider our generation of video viewers, the independent mind-set, and the appeal of convenience. Perhaps Barna recognized a few of these traits in his work *Revolution,* or perhaps Internet churches will be passing blimps on the radar screens of Christianity. That depends on whether Christian leaders and communicators embrace or reject this new form of "gathering." Will virtual gathering one day replace the local church?

Here's the crux of the issue—no matter the size of the church, no matter the servant, no matter the length of service, church leaders must understand that we are building the kingdom of God. Not our own kingdoms. The way we build the kingdom is one life at a time. It happens through the ministries of our local kingdom outposts— our churches. We must regain a New Testament understanding of church. We must battle the culture of consumerism with a dose of Philippians 2. We must battle the selfishness of materialism with the principle of eternal perspective. We must offset the by-product of competition and feelings of pride by esteeming others better than ourselves and maintaining the humility modeled by Christ.

We need leaders bold enough to stand against the tide and say, "Though I am but one, I will not give in to this culture." If God will raise up enough leaders bold enough to stand, then one by one, we will have an army cooperating for God's kingdom that can overcome the Evil One of this world.

Looking to the Future

The final question that we wish for those involved in the multisite-church movement to consider is one that each local congregation should ask: "Who chooses the pastor when the current one moves on or retires?" This may be the point that separates some of these congregations from others. But what will happen should there not be agreement over the new pastor? Will the sites wither away and die like Montgomery Ward or KMart in some regions? Will onetime megachurches be constant reminders of a failed religious experiment? Will the sites go through the process of separating from the founding church through court battles and property settlements? What witness will this provide for the church of Jesus Christ? Which site chooses the new pastor? What if one site decides it wants to live video stream a pastor from a different church because he is better than the new one at the current broadcast campus? Many questions and few answers lie ahead for the multisite movement. Far too much money and too many resources have been invested into a system filled with potential hazards.

If you must embark on the multisite journey, perhaps these suggestions at minimizing problems will help you:

1) Establish each location in such a way that if the campus wishes to separate from the founding location at a later time, it can do so without going to court.

2) Take steps to minimize personality building and consumer-driven churches.

3) Have several events a year where all members are invited to one location for services.

4) Allow each location to have some level of congregational control.

5) Mentor at least one person at all times who has the ability to take over one of the multisites or plant a church.

6) Support at least one church plant for every multisite location started.

Our inclination is that the multisite methodology should be feared rather than commended. It typically creates a consumer mentality, undermines church planting, compromises ecclesiology, and focuses on numerical growth as a measure of success. Churches currently involved in the multisite movement can develop exit strategies to give independence to those sites. Sites built on community and service to Christ will be able to survive and perhaps even thrive, resulting in newly planted churches. Locations built on a personality or the entertainment-driven model are not healthy churches anyway. While recognizing this criticism rings truer with the most ambitious forms of the multisite movement, every church leader should consider the lasting implications. The most important question is, "Why not plant new, independent churches for God's kingdom?"

DRIVE THRU

I'll Take That to Go

- Planting new churches rather than embarking on multisite locations should be an option considered.

- If you choose to start multisite locations, do so in a way that allows separation without a public court battle.

- Dynamic leaders have a responsibility to challenge members to consider full-time ministry and then to invest in those called out under their preaching.

- Attempt to promote others and replicate yourself rather than continuously building ministries centered on you.

- We are not called to steal sheep from another undershepherd; we are called to find lost sheep.

- Faithful preachers in small congregations can serve the Lord just as faithfully as preachers in large congregations.

Health Inspector

- When your church begins to grow, what determines the next steps you take?

- What are you doing to consistently call out and invest in others so that they can one day lead congregations?

- If you start a multisite location, have you allowed for that congregation to vote and withdraw from the founding campus? If not, then why not?

- Are you excited or do you become uneasy when a member from another nearby church suddenly wants to join your church? Is your first thought, "We must be better" or "How long before this person leaves here disgruntled as well?" Are either of these fair?

- What steps have you taken to encourage a small-church pastor in your area?

CHAPTER NINE

Expanding the Franchise:
Extending Your Brand or the Kingdom's?

Dave prayed passionately for his congregation for months. After years of rapid growth, the church plateaued. Every time it approached the next numerical hurdle, a few key families would be transferred or move, leading the church to rebuild again.

While Dave was deep in thought, the phone rang in his office. His face registered a look of pleasant surprise. Brent, the teaching pastor from a regional megachurch, was on the other end. At one time Brent served with Dave at Hexler Street Community Church, but now he served The Pinnacle Church.

"My senior pastor, Sean, wants to meet with you," Brent said. "He has a new vision for expanding the ministries of The Pinnacle on your side of town. Would you be interested?"

"Sure," Dave replied. After talking with another large church in the area about Hexler Street becoming a campus of its ministry, Dave thought The Pinnacle might be interested as well. While the talks with the other church had broken down, perhaps this new focus could be what would propel Dave's ministry forward.

Eventually Dave and the pastor of The Pinnacle settled on a date to meet. Over the next couple of weeks, Dave began to mull this over in his mind. What would it mean to become a campus of a larger congregation? What would his people think? Would they be replacing some of the good things happening with levels of bureaucracy, or could it help them reach more of the community?

The more Dave wrestled with the ideas, the more he struggled. He cared deeply about the people he shepherded. Was there something more to church life than being a franchise of a church across town? But could they actually reach more people as a satellite than as an independent congregation?

The Plans for Expansion

"So why not expand?" I (Thomas) asked. I owned and operated a very successful karate school for a few years. Starting the school at age eighteen had been a challenge, but I succeeded. Some of the success stemmed from winning the state championship, which carried name recognition in the sport. As with any business, I had to expand the school in order to keep expanding the number of students and the amount of income. So I launched another school far enough away not to draw students from my founding location but close enough that I could be present on occasion.

The result was that I began to rely more and more on my upper-level students and employees to help with day-to-day operations while I was "present" at the other location. I remember the thought crossing my mind: "What if one of my black belts went across the street and started a competing karate school?" The thought should have never crossed my mind. My students possessed great loyalty. But I already felt the rising territorial jealousy of wanting to be in charge.

When God called me to seminary, I sold the founding location to one of my top students. I did not know how he would do. He did not have the awards or all the flashy moves. He had something different. He possessed different abilities. I watched him grow into the challenging new role and flourish as the owner and head instructor of the school. Every time he invited me back for a class or test, I felt a greater sense at having had part in something that outlasted me.

I learned a valuable lesson. I had underestimated the ability of those around me. They rose to the challenge and excelled when they needed to do so. But I had to let them go in order to let them grow.

Undermining Church Planting

Multicampus churches know they want to reach more people with the good news. They know the current statistics about where people in America are. They have done their homework. Most multicampus congregations also know what works on their main campus and believe their core strategies will work no matter where applied.

But is there collateral damage from their choices? Could their growth actually undermine church plants or smaller churches in the area seeking to do the same thing the multisite congregation is attempting?

Financial Support

One proper way to utilize the multisite movement may be as a church-planting technique, but this takes an entirely different focus than most multisite ventures. Wayne Cordeiro, senior pastor of New Hope Christian Fellowship in Honolulu, stated, "Our goal for satellites is not necessarily to add locations. It is to develop new leaders. It is to edge these emerging leaders into their own teaching, where one day we can release them as stand-alone churches."[1] This method focuses on planting new churches and releasing control of these churches as soon as they are able to stand on their own. If a church feels that it must maintain control in order for the new church to be successful, then one must ask to whom the church belongs and who determines success. Are we more concerned about building earthly kingdoms than God's kingdom, and is that the reason control must be maintained?

There are some churches such as Capitol Hill Baptist Church in Washington, D.C., and Wedgwood Baptist Church in Fort Worth, Texas, that have decided to help revitalize struggling churches. These two churches have given resources, members, and in some cases staff to help other churches without control over budget, members, or other decisions. These are hard choices, but the end results have been positive, all while demonstrating the spirit of Christian brotherhood. Admittedly, not all multisite churches are equal in their structure, ambition, and scope. Some multisite churches also engage in church planting and give heavily to the global mission's effort. However, these criticisms ring true with the most ambitious and far-reaching models.

Lack of Cooperation

Wendy's was the first chain to introduce a 99-cent menu. The restaurant hoped to lure people in for the cheap items and then to encourage them to buy more expensively priced items while in the store. The strategy worked well. In fact, the strategy worked so well that other fast-food giants had to follow—competition demanded it. Taco Bell developed the value menu. Burger King and McDonald's also developed a 99-cent menu.[2] With Wendy's original move to the 99-cent menu, the fast-food wars began. McDonald's and Burger King could not afford to allow Wendy's to take market share by offering the value menu. With independent kingdoms each out for their own interest, nothing else could be expected.

Unfortunately, the church sometimes acts like the business world. Instead of finding cooperation even among like-minded and associated groups, competition between churches rules the day. Ultimately consumerism drives the competition for market shares. One church begins to offer Awana on Wednesday nights, and other churches that don't offer the program notice attendance declining in parents with children. Within months the program has spread into all the neighboring churches until the program no longer attracts new people because of its commonality. Along comes another new program, and the cycle repeats.

These programs attract adults also. DivorceCare, moms' morning out, women's Bible studies, men's groups, and other programs, including recreation teams, often draw members who normally do not attend but become consumers of these products being offered. If these members assimilate into the community, then perhaps the strategy worked. But often those attracted by programs never move past consumer status. When this happens, the consumers simply go to other churches with more products when the current church fails to offer the proper variety or something for a specific desire.

In other cases, one church accepts those disciplined by another church without ever inquiring into the action taken. Totally independent church actions mimic separate franchises in the business world. Christian unity should be different. Churches of like faith and practice should be able to hold joint events to spread the gospel. We should uphold the discipline of sister churches. We should work together to strengthen the kingdom of God, praying for sister churches and hoping for their well-being. We should be able to send members to struggling churches to revitalize them. We should be able to join together in planting churches and supporting missionaries without jealousy over numbers, influence, or budgets.

Multisite Foundation—in Scripture or Not?

This movement, while new, has not had many proponents attempt to find a scriptural basis for its existence. Most have pragmatically adopted the model based on the success of increased numbers. As one advocate stated, concerning an attempt at establishing a biblical foundation, "I found this very refreshing since many of those promoting multisite don't seem to have wrestled with the biblical implications of the approach … they only have a 'this works so it's got to be right and don't criticize me or slow me down with the Bible' kind of attitude."[3] However, a few have sought to find some scriptural backing for the multisite-church movement. Let's examine this effort and address some of the other problems this model may encourage.

Scriptural Foundation for Multisite

Acts 2

The search for scriptural evidence to support the multisite movement began in Acts 2. Some have argued that Acts 2 lays the biblical foundation for the multicampus church.[4] We have searched through Acts, looking for this foundation, but we remain unconvinced that it exists. Neither of us has a dog in this fight nor an axe to grind. We would just as soon find the scriptural support for the multicampus movement as not find it. In fact, it would be easier on us to discover support because many of our friends who serve as pastors currently use this methodology. However, we find little if any support for the multicampus movement in Acts. Let's review the argument and then look to see what Scripture states.

There are six points to the argument that we will discuss:

1) The Jerusalem church had a massive growth problem.

2) The Jerusalem church remained as one church.

3) That church devoted itself to the apostles' teaching.

4) There is no way the church could have been gathered as one large group.

5) In addition to smaller temple gatherings, the one church met in multiple houses every day to devote itself to the apostles' teaching.

6) The Jerusalem megachurch had massive organization problems and members who felt "left out."

Let's begin with the easy part. No one would disagree that the Jerusalem church experienced sudden, massive growth. Acts 2:41 states that about "three thousands souls" were added. However, larger growth occurred in Acts 4:4 as "the number of the men came to be about five thousand." This second record does not explicitly state that an additional five thousand were added, but that the number of men came to be about five thousand. This records only the number of men, which means that the estimated number of new believers was around five to ten thousand. These verses establish that the church at Jerusalem did experience sudden, massive growth, which establishes a precedent that megachurches are not new and not wrong.

We also agree with points two and three. The Jerusalem church did remain one church. We have no record to indicate the church split into many churches. In addition, Acts 2:46 (NKJV) states that they "continu[ed] daily with one accord in the temple," and the singular version of the Greek word for church is used when referring to Jerusalem as in Acts 8:1; 11:22; and 15:4. Acts 2:42 states that the new believers devoted themselves "to the apostles' teaching and to fellowship, to the breaking of bread and to prayer."

Scripture seems to indicate that the church did gather as one large group. In addition, Scripture does not provide an exact number of members. In Acts 2:5 we see that the crowd contained "Jews ... from every nation." We do not know if they remained in Jerusalem or eventually left. The only update on numbers simply states that the number grew to five thousand men. We have no knowledge of women or children who may have been members. The maximum number listed by proponents is ten thousand people. In Acts 2 and 3, we know they gathered together in the area known as Solomon's Porch. Acts 5:12 states, "And they were all with one accord in Solomon's portico."

Could Solomon's Porch hold five to ten thousand people? Solomon's Porch ran along the eastern wall of the temple, which was 1,509 feet in length.[5] To put this in perspective, the Bank of America stadium in Charlotte, North Carolina, measures only nine hundred feet in length and eight hundred feet wide. This stadium holds 73,367 people.[6] Admittedly, this is a stadium with seats, and the comparison is for example only. The wall would be about the length of five football fields. Also remember that this was the location where the three thousand were added and where the number increased to five thousand. Thus, we know that large crowds could gather and could hear from this location. This structure was enormous, and despite the lack of microphones or speakers, large crowds apparently had no trouble hearing. Biblical evidence forces the conclusion that even the large Jerusalem church could and did gather at Solomon's Porch.

Another area of confusion is that the Jerusalem church met in multiple houses every day to devote themselves to the apostles' teaching. I doubt this statement because Acts 2:44 states, "And all those who had believed were together." Acts 2:46 states, "Day by day continuing with one mind in the temple, and breaking bread from house to house, they were taking their meals together with gladness and sincerity of heart." These verses indicate that the believers were together for teaching and then separate for fellowship meals. It would have been problematic to have meals at Solomon's Portico, whereas standing and hearing oral sermons seems to have been the standard practice. The last point has little effect on the current discussion, but there is no disagreement that Acts 6 either establishes the office of deacon or demonstrates the embryonic form of this office.

The argument for multisite churches from Acts 2 comes from applying our current understanding to a different time and place. We cannot imagine standing for a sermon that has little to no amplification in a non-air-conditioned setting. The evidence presented to this point from Scripture for the multisite methodology is weak. It appears that Acts maintained a common gathering at the temple with smaller fellowship settings in homes. This method has been the traditional style of a large worship service for proclamation with small groups, home groups, or Sunday school classes for fellowship. We find no convincing evidence of the multisite methodology.

Acts 15 and the Jerusalem Council

The search for a scriptural foundation leads to Acts 15 and the Jerusalem council. The following demonstrates the logic: "You might say that the idea of 'one church, many locations' began with the persecution of the first Christ-followers in Jerusalem.... As the good news spread throughout Asia and into Europe, new congregations were formed, but they were all connected back to the church at Jerusalem as evidenced by the council that was held in Acts 15."[7] Does Acts 15 provide a biblical foundation for the multisite movement? The answer is no. Consider the following characteristics of Acts 15:

1) Paul and Barnabas were sent out by the church at Antioch and not Jerusalem. The church at Antioch independently sent them to Jerusalem to discuss a theological issue. The "original Jerusalem church" did not interject itself into the life of another congregation (Acts 15:2–3). Prior to this, Paul and Barnabas helped churches in Lystra, Iconium, and Antioch in appointing their own elders (Acts 14:21–25).

2) The Jerusalem council dealt with salvation by grace and requirements of the Mosaic law for circumcision (Acts 15:10–11).

3) The decision in Acts 15:22 indicates the "apostles and the elders, with the whole church" sent men to help settle the controversy.

4) The tone of the words sent from the Jerusalem council in Acts 15 encouraged the church to follow what Paul and Barnabas had said. The letter neither dictated action nor does it establish any type of multisite movement.

The effort to use Acts goes further when it is stated:

Paul and Barnabas discovered some of the organizational challenges of a multi-campus church very early on, as reflected in Acts 15. The Jerusalem campus felt that the other congregations just weren't doing things the way they were done at the "main campus," so several self-appointed leaders headed to Antioch to straighten them out. "This brought Paul and Barnabas into sharp dispute and debate with them" (Acts 15:2). Paul and Barnabas were appointed, along with some other church members, to go to Jerusalem to sort out this problem. At Jerusalem, they began working out organizational challenges, defining the essential DNA of the new church, and clarifying how best to communicate between the campuses.[8]

There is no reason to believe that members of the church in Jerusalem saw themselves as the "main campus" and no reason to believe that Paul and Barnabas saw themselves as establishing "multi-campus" churches that gave decision-making authority to Jerusalem. Paul instructed the church at Corinth to deal with church discipline when it was gathered and did not tell the church to contact Jerusalem to see how it should proceed.

Some have attempted to link the multisite movement to history "from mission stations to Methodist circuit riders to branch Sunday schools done by bus ministry."[9] In fact, Craig Groeschel, pastor of Life Church in Oklahoma City, states that "the move from horseback preacher to satellite broadcast is simply a shift from circuit rider to closed-circuit rider."[10] This reveals closely the link between the structure of the multisite to hierarchical denominations.

We find both the argument from Scripture and the argument from church history weak concerning the establishment of the multisite-church movement. The majority of those involved in the multisite movement do so out of sincere desire to reach as many people with the gospel as quickly as possible, but history also demonstrates that those who follow our current leaders usually take things one step further than the leaders would have. The current model moves into dangerous territory, and the precedent being established for future generations of leaders may be detrimental to the American church.

Church Planting: The Biblical Model

In the New Testament, planting churches was the plan to spread the gospel to the ends of the earth. The importance of the church can be seen in its establishment. Matthew 16:18 says, "upon this rock I will build My church; and the gates of Hades will not overpower it." In Jesus' final words recorded in the gospel of Matthew we see the Great Commission: "Go therefore and make disciples of all the nations, baptizing them in the name of the Father and the Son and the Holy Spirit, teaching them to observe all that I commanded you; and lo, I am with you always, even to the end of the age" (Matt. 28:19–20). We cannot fulfill the Great Commission without "teaching them" what Christ commanded. The teaching comes through the church. A similar concept arises in Acts 1:8: "You shall be My witnesses both in Jerusalem, and in all Judea and Samaria, and even to the remotest part of the earth."

When the disciples witnessed about Christ, the converts met together and formed churches. Paul planted churches wherever he went. He left individuals to set things in order. Titus 1:5 says, "For this reason I left you in Crete, that you would set in order what remains and appoint elders in every city as I directed you." The book of Revelation contains letters to seven churches. Acts 20:28 tells us that God purchased the church with His own blood. Ephesians 3:10 states "that the manifold wisdom of God might now be made known through the church to the rulers and the authorities in the heavenly places." The church is the body and the bride. When Saul persecutes the church in Jerusalem, Christ says, "Saul, Saul, why are you persecuting Me?" The church is very important to Christ. If the church was God's plan, then we certainly cannot improve upon it.

Does planting churches solve the problems associated with the multisite-church movement? The answer to that question is yes *and* no. A new church plant can be just as consumer driven as an existing church. But a church plant usually avoids many issues such as:

1)   Church plants avoid consumerism of entertaining speakers.

2)   Church plants avoid compromising congregational polity.

3)   Church plants avoid sacrificing local church autonomy.

4)   Church plants allow other leaders to develop and excel.

5)   Church plants allow us to multiply disciples.

We must plant biblical churches. Once that occurs, the process of multiplication can have a greater impact than simple addition.

Misplaced Multiplication and Hostile Takeovers

Remember Dave, pastor of Hexler Street Community Church? He really wrestled with what was best for the future of his church—as many pastors do. When several large churches began talking to him about potentially joining with them, it fed his ego and his desire to be a part of something successful. Ultimately, that's why he agreed to meet with Sean, the senior pastor of The Pinnacle. While the names have been changed to protect the churches involved, Dave's story is true.

As Dave shut the door of his car in the parking lot, his apprehension grew about meeting with Sean. He entered the restaurant and found Brent, the teaching pastor, standing inside. Slightly confused, Dave asked if Sean could still make the meeting. Brent nodded and pointed to a table across the room. Sean stood and waved. At least eight other guys stood as well. As Dave moved toward the table, Sean beckoned him to take the empty chair next to him and then introduced the senior staff of The Pinnacle. This made Dave feel a little uneasy. What happened to a simple lunch with the pastor?

After the introductions, Sean made small talk with Dave for a short time but then turned to the subject at hand.

"We would like you to lead your congregation to become our West Campus."

Dave felt ambushed. Here he sat in front of the entire senior staff of one of the largest churches in the area, and the pastor wanted him to simply lead his congregation in a new direction?

Dave balked a bit. He wasn't ready for this like he'd thought.

"What would be my role?" he asked.

"I guess we could give you a Sunday school class, if you'd like," Sean replied. "Besides, your Sunday morning class would have more people in it than your regular church attendance now."

Dave grew quiet. From that point on, he didn't feel like eating or talking anymore. There was no concern for the people he had grown to love. There was no concern for the work God had done. There was no concern for his role as a minister.

Questions began to focus on acreage, buildings, numbers, attendance, and how well the congregation would accept a video sermon each week.

Dave finally left the meeting. He told Sean there was no way his church would be interested in this type of merging.

In the back of Dave's mind, the stories of the latest multicampus satellite in his community were coming back to haunt him. Stories of how the struggling congregation sought help from a larger, out-of-state church. How promises were made, but as soon as the ink dried on the "merger," the smaller church found itself with a new staff, as the current staff did not fit the image of the multicampus church. Offerings no longer went to needs in the local community but were deposited into a centralized account and redistributed as the main campus over three hundred miles away deemed best. Current property was sold, and the church relocated to an old movie theater. The multimillion-dollar slice of land the smaller church had bought years ago was put up for sale, netting the out-of-state church a handsome sum. Since the multicampus congregation in the community had dwindled below 150 in weekly attendance, the campus may be closing its doors.

The sales pitches continue all over the nation. Regional multisite churches may offer your smaller church a way "in." "Your congregation should merge with ours and become the north campus of our congregation!" The solicitation comes laden with promises of the latest technology, the best communicator piped in via video, nearly unlimited resources, and all at a seemingly low cost. Bite, and your church loses its identity to a large conglomerate, where everyday decisions are made by a pastor or leadership team in another city that doesn't know your local community. You just became a franchise of the Big Church in Someplace, USA.

Think it won't happen to your church? Think again. All across America churches are discovering ways to "resource share" as one small church after another closes its doors. One of the larger multisite congregations, LifeChurch.tv, offers congregations a portal on its Web page where interested church members can contact the leadership of LifeChurch about merging (they call it uniting) with their ministries and becoming a satellite.[11] Even Ed Young Jr. and his CreativePastors.com Web site inform churches that "Fellowship Church is continually expanding its borders and making greater impact with the message of Christ. If your church is interested in reaching more people and would be open to merging with Fellowship Church, then let us know."[12]

What are we building? A brand? A franchise? A marketed name? Some churches like Saddleback that have been slow to jump on the multicampus bandwagon are now offering churches in California the opportunity to "merge" with their campus and project Rick Warren's sermons every week.

On a theological level, are we creating future problems for our congregations? What happens when the pastor leaves? Many multicampus structures feature the teaching of just one person at all campuses. Will people stay when his ministry tenure is over, or will someone simply place his sermon series in rerun? Since the main campus holds the deed to all properties held in most multicampus structures, what determines the viability of each location? In a transition between leaders, how do you chose? Are certain campuses given more priority?

According to Dr. Gene Getz, two major issues concern him about many satellite-driven churches. The first issue has to do with the sense of community created by campus pastors. In his perspective, multicampus churches must invest in the best men they can find to be campus pastors, or they "may not have dynamic community needed to sustain the location." Part of that campus pastor's job must center on building strong relationships with members. Without that, how can a satellite campus ever reach many of the needs that community has. "Who visits the sick? Who marries? Who conducts funerals?" All of these elements are part of the responsibilities of the pastor. When the connection is between the attendee and the video screen, satellite-campus pastors must work overtime to connect with the people.

The second issue Getz worries about is the way many multiple-location churches build their ministries around a single pastor. "What happens when a pastor passes off the scene? If the only pastor broadcast via video to locations across the satellite structure is a single pastor, a serious complication could occur in his absence." Churches must disciple and develop new leaders carefully while thinking about the future of the congregation.

Dr. Getz warns all leaders that the work of Christ "must be built by sharing and mentoring other leaders." When it came time for. Getz to transition from his role as pastor of Fellowship Bible Church, he stated that it was "a thrill to pass on the ministry to the young men I discipled." Even in the final years of his senior pastor role at Fellowship Bible North (now Chase Oaks Church), Getz made certain to train the pastor who replaced him. Creating a unique seven-year transfer strategy, Jeff Jones, Getz's replacement at Chase Oaks, eventually took on the ministry halfway through the process. "Jeff started by teaching 50 percent of time. By the time we were ready to pass the baton, people were excited."[13]

A positive approach to the multiplication principle can be summarized in the oft-used illustration "Give a man a fish and you have fed him for a day. Teach a man to fish and you have fed him for a lifetime." Planting new churches does not come without problems and does not happen easily. It does, however, avoid many problems associated with the multisite methodology, and it gives a place for the training and discipling of new leaders.

So the questions still remain: Are multicampus congregations still functioning as churches, or have they crossed into a new category? Are some of these multisite churches creating modern, centralized McDenominations? In the next chapter, we will address some of the issues of the denominational structure that some of the multicampus congregations begin to possess.

DRIVE THRU ⬆

I'll Take That to Go

- ▫ Financial resources dedicated to the multisite movement unintentionally undermine support of church plants.

- ▫ When churches in close proximity compete with each other, it undermines the unity of brothers and sisters in Christ and creates independent kingdoms rather than focusing on God's kingdom.

- ▫ While scriptural evidence for the multisite movement is scarce, scriptural evidence for the importance of planting churches is abundant.

- ▫ Pastors must disciple and train the next generation of leaders. This goes beyond the training they receive at seminary.

- ▫ Moving away from a centralized role, the pastor can enable the future ministry of the church.

Health Inspector

- ▫ What is your church doing to plant a church?

- ▫ How could planting a church help your congregation be more kingdom focused?

- ▫ Do you pray publicly for other congregations in your town? Why or why not?

- ▫ How do you feel when God uses other congregations near you?

CHAPTER TEN

The Coming of McDenominations: How Multisite Strategies May Bring the End of Church Autonomy

> Fourteen thousand members and me,
> Watch the preacher up on the screen,
> I have never shaken his hand,
> My two-dimensional pastor-man.
> —"Happy," Ross King, *Welcome to America*[1]

◻ Well over fifteen hundred churches are already multisite.

◻ One out of four megachurches is holding services at multiple locations.

◻ One out of three churches says it is thinking about developing an additional service in a new location.

◻ Seven out of the country's ten fastest-growing churches offer worship in multiple locations, as do nine of the ten largest churches.[2]

You probably already got the memo. We aren't too keen on the multicampus-church movement. You are wondering, "Why would you want to pour water on this fiery multisite movement that seems to be reaching people for the gospel?" Why offer theological critiques? Why not just be passionate about evangelism and allow all methods that work to be used? These are valid questions, and we can assure you that this book is not an academic fire truck intent on putting out any spiritual fire.

Despite our concerns, we assume that the motives for establishing a multisite church are noble and good, but good motives and intent do not always equal proper results. One book claims, "The primary motive behind the multisite approach is to obey the church's God-given directives. The Great Commandment (Matt. 22:37–39) is to love God and one another, the Great Commission (Matt. 28:18–20) is to make disciples of all nations, and the Great Charge (1 Peter 5:1–4) reminds us to involve all believers in ministry."[3] John Piper, a man whom we greatly respect, has embarked with a multisite methodology out of a sense of responsibility for reaching lost people.[4] These motives are noble and should be the desire of all Christians and all churches. The question for this discussion is not motive nor the validity of the Great Commandment, the Great Commission, or the Great Charge. The question is what impact this new methodology will have on American Christianity.

A multisite church is defined as a church that contends to be one local church and has multiple locations for meetings. As we begin this chapter, you should recognize the varieties of multisite churches. For example, some churches have only one off-campus site and a joint business meeting once a month. These efforts attempt to protect congregational polity and maintain one gathered congregation. These situations can hardly be compared to LifeChurch.tv, which has multiple locations in Oklahoma and others in Mesa, Arizona; Wellington, Florida; Albany, New York; Hendersonville, Tennessee; and Fort Worth, Texas.[5] In addition to these physical locations, the church has a "global internet campus" and a virtual campus in the world of Second Life.[6] Craig Groeschel, senior pastor of LifeChurch.tv stated in an interview with NBC, "When Jesus told us to go into all the world, we took Him very literally."[7] Perhaps it would be more accurate to say that LifeChurch.tv has taken Jesus virtually with an elaborate virtual church that plays music, allows you to fill out information cards and watch your choice of sermons, while virtually sitting in a facility identical to their real-world location. You can even partake of Communion with the rest of their Internet campus by simply bringing your own grape juice or Kool-Aid and saltine crackers to your computer screen.[8]

Why Address This Issue?

The widespread acceptance of this methodology deserves consideration. *The Multi-Site Church Revolution* states, "The approach of taking one church to multiple sites seems to be the beginning of a revolution in how church is done in North America and around the world."[9] The impact could be substantial. One author stated, "We predict that 30,000 American churches will be multi-site within the next few years, which means one or more multi-site churches will probably be in your area.… With one out of three churches seriously looking into multi-site, a revolution is afoot in how the church reaches new people for Christ."[10]

We see potential problems with this structure. This structure creates minidenominations, which remove local church autonomy. The plan centralizes power in the "main campus," and a centralized leadership negates congregational input. A recent book defined a multisite church as one that "shares a common vision, budget, leadership, and board."[11] A common budget, board, and leadership among multiple congregations creates problems. This chapter will focus on the effect the multisite movement could have on local church autonomy and local church government. If you are already involved in the multisite movement, this discussion should at the very least bring some potential perils to light and help you minimize those problems or redirect your plans.

As we begin this conversation, it will be beneficial to first define what a denomination is. The reasons for this will become apparent as we continue. We will briefly discuss the various forms of denominational and local church structure. After this summary, we will mention appropriate biblical principles for church structure and explain how this model may not meet the biblical standard. Lastly, we will attempt to point out some future implications that multisite churches will face.

What Is a Denomination?

Many characterize this age as "postdenominational," meaning either that independent churches and pastors have sprung up without loyalty to any particular group or that agencies outside the church seek to accomplish God's mission without denominational affiliation. But according to Merriam-Webster's dictionary, a denomination is, "a religious organization whose congregations are united in their adherence to its beliefs and practices."[12] Taking this definition, the multisite movement is establishing the age of the minidenomination. Each local church starting a multisite ministry with strongly connected ties back to one main or founding campus has created a minidenomination. While denominations positively signal cooperation for God's causes, the current phenomenon has problematic theological elements.

Interestingly, many of the churches struggling for identity in this postdenominational age come from what is called the "free church" tradition. As a brief reminder, the free-church tradition emphasizes the autonomy of the local congregation from any external organization. Additionally, free churches usually stress the priesthood of all believers to the extent that each member is an integral part of church organizational structure from voting on leadership (pastors, elders, deacons, church boards) to issues of building maintenance. This has led some denominations like Baptists to claim that they are not actually denominations, but simply associating churches.

One of the most problematic elements of the multisite movement is the forfeiture of local church autonomy. The breakdown of the free-church structure, along with its basic theological commitments, leads to other theological issues. The local congregation has given up the right to decide major decisions, placing that authority in the main campus. We do not mean the color of the carpet or how often the lightbulbs should be changed. The decisions at question are (1) the ability to elect the officers of the church usually called pastors and deacons, (2) the ability to accept members into the congregation, (3) the ability to exclude members from the congregation, and (4) the ability to vote on the use of budgetary funds.

Historically, free churches insist on the freedom to do what the members of that particular congregation decide, so long as it coincides with the law of Christ. In contrast to the free-church movement, other well-established denominations control many aspects of the local body, including externally selecting the pastor. Only a handful of these top-down organizations currently participate in the multisite movement.[13] To date, no one has clearly researched the shortage of hierarchical denominations that participate in the multicampus-ministry models. Yet a simple answer may be found in that a hierarchical structure would require church plants rather than allowing one church in the system the ability to create an authority structure beneath it. Perhaps the theology behind the hierarchical ecclesiology prevents more churches from participating. Until the multisite movement grows and further research is available, theories are all we have. Before we begin, it might be helpful to provide a summary of the various types of church government indicating the structure that lends itself to participation in the multisite movement.

Summary of Denominational Structures[14]

Top-Down Structure (Hierarchical Structure)

The Episcopal system represents one system that operates from the top down and functions in a similar fashion to the Roman Catholic Church. Thus, if the General Assembly made a decision to ordain homosexual ministers, the local churches would be forced to follow instructions or work through the system to reverse the decision.[15] At the top of the system, an archbishop governs many bishops, who have authority over a "diocese" or set number of churches in a given area. Each local parish within the diocese has a rector or vicar (assistant or substitute for the rector) responsible for decision making. All of these officers have been ordained into the Episcopal priesthood. In this

structure, decisions come from the top down. This can be problematic for some local congregations when the organization affirms Gene
Robinson as a homosexual minister and elects a woman, Katharine
Jefferts Schori, as presiding bishop.[16] The local congregations have
no recourse for action other than withdrawal from the organization,
which means losing the property and buildings or reaching an agreement for payment.

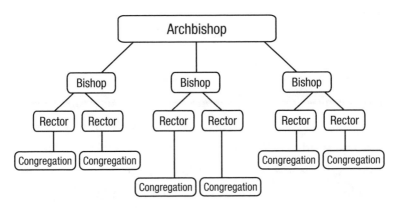

Complete Independence (Bible Church) Model

In addition to the top-down model, another variation of church government exists that is totally independent. This method of church
government demonstrates minimal cooperation between portions of
the churches usually for specifically stated purposes. These churches
possess complete independence except from the laws of Christ in the
New Testament. These independent churches own their own property, use budget money without outside input, elect church officers,
accept members, and discipline members. No uniform organizational
chart exists, but if one were formed, it might look something like an
ecclesiological petri dish.

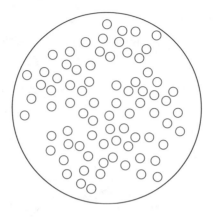

Free-Church Structures

In between the independent model and the top-down model exists a different model that has many variations. Some churches that call themselves independent cooperate with various fellowships—for example, the Baptist Bible Fellowship. These churches have an organized form of cooperation and yet maintain all the decision-making liberty of the independent model. The largest Baptist denomination in the world possesses the most advanced form of this structure. The churches in the Southern Baptist Convention still retain complete autonomy and the benefits of decision-making authority that independent churches or churches of fellowships possess. The primary difference lies in the level of cooperation. Specifically, Southern Baptists utilize what is called the "cooperative program" to finance missions, theological education, and church-planting efforts. This system is the most effective of any independent cooperative model. The Southern Baptist Convention (and others included in this group) operates with a cooperative spirit that works from the bottom up. The organization is held together by a "rope of sand as strong as steel." Each local congregation owns its own property and possesses autonomy. The final decision remains in the local church. The extent of the involvement of the congregation varies, but in most of these churches, the congregations elect church officers, control their own budgets, accept members, and discipline members. No church, association, or convention has the authority to infringe upon the decision-making ability of any congregation. This structure operates with the local church, local associations, state conventions, and a national convention. Because the cooperation is voluntary, some local congregations bypass either the local associations or the state convention and participate only with the national convention. Cooperation is typically defined by monetary investment into the mission of the convention and agreement with its purposes.

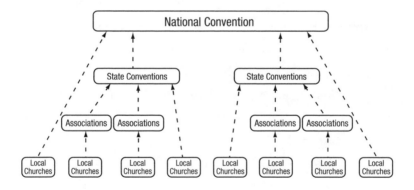

The Network Method

A new model has emerged from Saddleback Church with a network of "purpose-driven ministries." A similar model can be found with Willow Creek and the network of those in the Willow Creek Association. Although these networks would appear to be denominations in and of themselves, they claim members from multiple traditional denominations. For example, the Willow Creek Web site states, "The WCA is a not-for-profit ministry with more than 11,000 Member Churches from 90 denominations and 45 countries."[17] The main requirement is not cooperation for ministry but a membership fee of $249 per year. For this you receive the benefits of membership, a discount on resources, and subscription to a magazine.[18] The Saddleback model of purpose-driven ministries and the PEACE plan offer multiple levels of cooperation. The primary thing offered is service, and the primary requirement is a joining fee. No confession of faith binds these churches together. The primary binding force is the desire to consume the goods offered by "the network provider."

This could be compared to a wireless network. One computer may be connected to the wireless network in order to benefit from its provision. Another computer in close proximity may be connected to the network and the two computers never connected to each other. They could connect to each other as well, but that is not necessary. In addition, the wireless network cannot download anything to the computer unless the user agrees to it. Thus, you have a truly independent consumer mentality with minimal connectivity. While one consumer may be connected all day every day, another may connect periodically, and some seldom, if ever, connect to the resources of the network. The model might look something like the following illustration. The dotted lines represent the minimal amount of connectedness, but a consumer-based denomination has resulted from these networks.

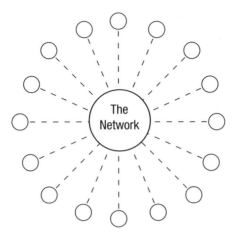

The Multisite Structure

The multisite-church phenomenon has brought a new structure reminiscent of the days of blossoming denominations. The structure begins with the "original church," which some may refer to as the "mother church, sending church, home church, or main campus"; however, this terminology is not preferred by proponents.[19] These original churches establish off-campus sites that they control because they own the property, determine the staff, and control the budget. The off-campus sites may be something as simple as a few people watching a delayed video in a local school or as complex as thousands watching live streaming video in a multimillion-dollar facility. The off-campus locations may be just around the corner, or they may be thousands of miles away. As the following graphic demonstrates, these original churches resemble the denominational headquarters for a newly started minidenomination. The one exception being that the denominational headquarters is a church itself.

Big circles represent
the original church.

Little circles represent the various sites.
The lines represent the connection.

The Multisite Church Structure

This system clearly falls within the top-down system of government. In fact, control over the other sites is one benefit some see to this. "The power and synergy of an interconnected network of churches held together through vision and values is far more greater than the segmentation and disconnectedness of our present system."[20]

Another benefit comes through the control of monetary funds. Scott Reavely, pastor of New Life Church near Portland, Oregon, claims that this approach "provides far more flexibility than being an independent church plant would. 'Emotionally, there was significant resistance to saying goodbye to people we've known for many years, and financially, it would be devastating to send out a large portion of our givers.... Now I feel free to encourage my best givers and best workers to go to our new sites without fear that we as the sending location will never recover.'"[21]

Working as a top-down system of government, the home church

controls all phases of the off-campus site, including the content of the Sunday morning worship and even the selection of songs at some locations. This structuring of the service helps maintain the branding or predictability necessary to ensure similar worship experiences no matter the location. While some see this as necessary, this level of control cannot be found throughout history and most closely resembles liturgical methodology. In most cases, this structure eliminates the autonomy at the off-campus location, eliminates congregational government at the off-campus location, eliminates the electing of officers at the off-campus location, and eliminates the control of funds given by the off-campus location.

Is this problematic? Yes, if these principles are biblical, which we believe they are. With that in mind, we will now look at the biblical evidence for these principles. If Scripture indicates that these principles should be supported as Baptists and other free-church congregations have historically held, then the question becomes do you follow the teaching of Scripture or the next church-growth technique?

Biblical Principles for Church Structure

Scripture does not clearly establish a complete church structure with every detail outlined. Thus, this discussion will mention principles and examples given in Scripture that have historically been used by free churches to defend their structure. At the very least, Scripture teaches that the local church has the right to choose its leaders, exclude members, and admit members.

Scripture indicates that the local church has the right to elect its own leaders. The first example of this comes from Acts 6:3–5:

> "Brethren, *select from among you* seven men of good reputation, full of the Spirit and of wisdom, whom we may put in charge of this task. But we will devote ourselves to prayer and to the ministry of the word." And the statement found *approval with the whole congregation*; and *they chose* Stephen, a man full of faith and of the Holy Spirit, and Philip, Prochorus, Nicanor, Timon, Parmenas and Nicolas, a proselyte from Antioch.

This passage demonstrates that the apostles did not choose the men who served as embryonic deacons. This surely would have been much simpler than allowing the majority to determine its own leaders. However, the apostles themselves instructed the multitude to choose out from among them their leaders. John Calvin also affirmed the authority of the congregation to elect its elders.[22] Additional evidence can be found in Acts 15:22: "Then it seemed good to the apostles and the elders, *with the whole church*, to choose men from among them to send to Antioch with Paul and Barnabas—Judas called Barsabbas, and Silas, leading men among the brethren." The apostles made the decision with the "whole church." In the majority of cases in the multisite movement, the off-campus congregation has little or no say into who serves as its officers. The original church determines the staff and controls the staff. Thus, staff members report to the original church and not to the local congregation.

Scripture indicates that the local church has the right to exclude members from its fellowship. Jesus Himself, in Matthew 18:15–17, established the rules to be followed and the right of a congregation to discipline members. It states:

> If your brother sins, go and show him his faults in private; if he listens to you, you have won your brother. But if he does not listen to you, take one or two more with you, so that by the mouth of two or three witnesses every fact may be confirmed. If he refuses to listen to them, tell it to the church; and if he refuses to listen even to the church, let him be to you as a Gentile and a tax collector.

In addition to Matthew 18, the right of a church to dismiss members was given 1 Corinthians 5:4–5 and 13.

> In the name of our Lord Jesus, *when you are assembled*, and I with you in spirit, with the power of our Lord Jesus, I have decided to deliver such a one to Satan for the destruction of his flesh, so that his spirit may be saved in the day of the Lord Jesus…. But those who are outside, God judges. Remove the wicked man *from among yourselves*.

These three verses indicate that the local assembly or church has the duty and responsibility to exclude members. These verses do not say to appeal to elders, to send the decision to an outside body, but for the local church when it assembles to deal with the issue. Most multisite churches will never assemble together at one time. Thus, the biblical example cannot be followed unless each individual congregation possesses the right to discipline.

Scripture indicates that the local church has the right to admit members into its fellowship. Romans 14:1 states, "Now accept the one who is weak in faith, but not for the purpose of passing judgment on his opinions." This book is written to "all that be in Rome, beloved of God, called to be saints." Paul instructed this group to accept the one. Another example of the authority of the church to accept members comes from the New Testament example of church discipline given in 2 Corinthians. After church discipline had worked successfully, Paul urged the church at Corinth to allow a member back into its fellowship. Second Corinthians 2:6 indicates that the punishment was inflicted by the "many." This implied the rule of the majority of the church. Furthermore, in 2 Corinthians 2:6–8 Paul urged the church to reaffirm its love to the offender. Lastly, if the church has the power to exclude members and to admit excluded members, this implies the power to admit any applying members. Notice that in none of these examples does Scripture indicate that the church at Corinth should inquire of the church in Jerusalem about its actions.

Scripture indicates that these rights belong to the local church. Most in the free-church movement have historically defended this belief, which explains why they are in the free church category rather than a hierarchical denomination. However, when a "free church" decides to move toward multiple locations, usually the principles given by Scripture are compromised. The off-site location has no authority to select its own leaders, exclude members, or admit members. Part if not all of these tasks fall on the shoulders of the original church. Thus, the multisite movement stands the risk of jeopardizing local church autonomy and the scriptural decision-making ability of the local congregation.

McChurch and Its Problems

Perhaps we have convinced you that the multisite movement or McChurch in general tends to create problems. It creates a problem of traditional church structure, which history contends resulted from a biblical perspective. It creates a problem of encouraging entertainment mentality and consumerism. It creates a problem of content focused at the lowest common denominator with a message that offends as few as possible. If we have done our job, then some of you are thinking, "Okay, so I see your point, but how do I quit?" Now, that's a great question! We'll explore the subject in the next chapter.

DRIVE THRU ⬆

I'll Take That to Go

- Nine of the ten largest churches in America offer worship in multiple locations.

- There is a wide spectrum of ideas relating to how churches should create a multicampus structure.

- The approach of taking one church to multiple sites seems to be the beginning of a revolution in how church is done in North America and around the world.

- We predict some thirty thousand American churches will be multisite within the next few years, which means one or more multisite churches will probably be in your area.

- Multisite churches generally give up congregational government with the founding site making decisions for every other location.

- Multisite churches generally give up local church autonomy with every decision, including staff and budget, being made by the founding location.

- Multisite churches have created minidenominations with bishops leading the locations and directing the campus rectors.

Health Inspector

◘ Which church structure does your congregation follow? What are its inherent strengths and weaknesses?

◘ If your church comes from a free-church tradition, is it worth changing your church government to adopt the multisite methodology? Why or why not?

◘ How can multisite churches practice church discipline as an assembly?

CHAPTER ELEVEN

Quitting McChurch

It caught the corner of my eye. I (Thomas) turned and looked at the rectangular implement as though it contained leprosy. I had avoided it every morning for the past year. I did not fear catching a disease. I dreaded the truth of judgment—with a similar feeling to a checkup at the dentist office. This morning was different. No more excuses. I had finished my classes. The deadlines that come with a PhD had ended, and now my poor health choices were showing.

I told myself that my lack of exercise lasted for a season of life. I told myself that fast food allowed more time to study. The truth of the matter was that I like the food. The food was good, and the service was impeccable. For more than a year, I had ignored long-term consequences. Instead, I enjoyed the immediate gratification of a double Quarter Pounder with cheese, fries, and a chocolate shake. I enjoyed it so much that I ate some sort of fast food at least twice week, if not three times.

With no excuses left, I stepped on the scales of justice, knowing the consequences would not be pleasant. I watched with anticipation as the numbers registered a twenty-pound gain. I couldn't believe it. I have seen those models of what ten pounds of fat looked like, and now my immediate gratification had turned into twenty pounds of unwanted excess baggage. I couldn't really blame anyone but myself. I consciously knew it an unwise decision to pull up to the drive-through. And yet despite the blame lying clearly at my feet, I could not help but feel as though I had been wronged in some way.

I was a consumer. I desired a product that did me no favors. I made bad life choices, and now I had to deal with the consequences. In order to rectify the situation, I would have to work out, eat less, and make better choices. As I pondered how this had happened, I began to ask questions that had never crossed my mind before. How many calories did that food contain? Should McDonald's feel bad in any way about feeding my obsession for unhealthy food? Is there not someone who would keep them accountable for making bad choices so easy?

Curiosity drove me to the Internet. I looked, and to my amazement the double Quarter Pounder contains 740 calories, the large fries another 570, and the triple-thick 21-ounce chocolate shake another 770 calories.[1] I added up the intake of my simple, enjoyable trip to discover that more than once a week for over a year, I had consumed 2,080 calories in one quick trip. I wish someone had stopped me along the way and said, "What are doing to yourself? Slow down a little, and think about the long-term consequences."

To put my calorie intake into perspective, a six-inch turkey sub contains 280 calories.[2] One hour of walking at 3.5 mph would burn 346 calories for a person of my weight.[3] One hour of high-impact aerobics would burn 637 calories for a person of my weight.[4] I would have to walk for six hours to burn off the calories from one lunch. I would have to participate in over three hours of high-impact aerobics. When making the decision for immediate gratification, I did not think that what I ate in fifteen minutes would take six hours of walking or three hours of aerobics to reverse.

My trips to McDonald's had been enjoyable, but had they been beneficial? Immediately, I found it gratifying; consequently, I found it horrifying. The scales of judgment rendered their verdict. I knew that I had to quit McDonald's and embark on a healthy lifestyle with long-term benefits.

The fast-food industry is not alone in taking advantage of immediate gratification. Credit card companies have mastered it. The "buy now, pay later" mentality feeds our obsession with materialism. Even lenders have indulged in the practice, resulting in historic levels of foreclosures as Americans have bought more than they can afford. Cash advance locations exist conveniently near you, and rent-to-own businesses operate with success. All of these businesses have determined to profit from our need for immediate gratification rather than encourage a healthier long-term plan. Even our government mortgages the future of the nation now by running up deficits, seemingly for immediate political popularity. Eventually the scales of justice may render a verdict in these areas, resulting in economic disaster for individuals, companies, or our country.

More importantly for this book, the church has bought into the concept. Our sermons must be entertaining, our locations must be convenient, and our music must be exciting. If the location is not convenient enough then offer Internet church to each person's own living room. If the message of the cross, the blood, or sin offends too harshly, then tone down the message, and speak motivationally about having your best life now. If theology gets in the way, then claim individual liberty, and allow everyone to have an equally valid yet completely contradictory true opinion. If one age-group wants hymns and another wants choruses, then provide two different services to meet the demands of the consumer. Let's make religion easy so that more people will participate.

One day, American Christians will wake up to the scales of spiritual justice and realize that our obsession with easy Christianity, while quick, convenient, and painless, has lost the essence of what Christianity is all about. The spiritual experience, while enjoyable, may have more benefit for immediate gratification than eternal reward.

Has the church pared away the superfluous mere traditionalism, or has is missed the very foundation of Christianity? Has it lost the essence of what it means to follow Christ for the sake of a consumer-driven, entertainment-fed experiment called McChurch? We have argued that we have compromised essentials of ecclesiology for the sake of the number of bodies, size of the building, and increasing of the budget. Not all have crossed the ambiguous line of commercialization, but some are teetering on the edge of the precipice and about to fall headlong into franchising McChurch. We hope by now some of you are wondering how we go about quitting McChurch or what can we do to prevent the fall. In the remainder of this chapter, we will discuss two categories where some changes can be made—one for the individual Christian and another for the church.

Quitting McChurch—the Individual's Decision in Eternal Perspective
The foundation of quitting McChurch on an individual level begins with an eternal perspective. As long as you live this life for what you can

get out of it, then you will never truly be able to change your consumer-driven, materialistic mentality. You must develop a mentality that lives for eternity. Heaven is your home. You are a pilgrim passing through this earth. Such a mentality affects every decision of your life.

Living for the now encourages immediate gratification. A bestselling book has even been written about how to live your best life now. Your perspective will affect decisions you make and how you view your spiritual relationship to Jesus Christ. If you desire to live your best life now, then Jesus becomes something of an add-on to an already good life. Let's face it, most Americans have it pretty good, historically speaking. However, even in the American life, there are moments of despair, frustration, and trials. Is it only during these moments that you really want religion or a God to fall back on? Religion becomes a crutch for times of need. When things go well, religion becomes like an added feature to a new car or the second vacation home. Religion adds to this experience called life in ways that fulfill and enrich but that do not cost you anything. Religion simply fills a need in Maslow's hierarchy. This mentality leads to uncommitted Christians whose names reside on church membership roles all across America but who only access their "insurance policy" when needed.

Let's contrast that with an eternal perspective. Immediate gratification and an eternal perspective are completely opposite. The New Testament tells believers to live with an eternal perspective. Jesus promises that His believers will have tribulation. Thus, a decision to follow Christ is a decision for trouble in this life with eternal rewards to follow. Jesus says in Matthew 5:10–12, "Blessed are those who have been persecuted for the sake of righteousness, for theirs is the kingdom of heaven. Blessed are you when people insult you and persecute you, and falsely say all kinds of evil against you because of Me. Rejoice, and be glad, for your reward in heaven is great, for in the same way they persecuted the prophets who were before you." Jesus promises that our reward comes in heaven and not on earth. John 16:33 says, "These things I have spoken to you, so that in Me you may have peace. In the world you have tribulation, but take courage; I have overcome the world." Christians are promised trouble in this world.

Even the casual reader of the New Testament understands that Christianity is a costly call—a call that requires devotion, obedience, and commitment. Perhaps the words of Luke 9:23–25 state it best: "And He was saying to them all, 'If anyone wishes to come after Me, he must deny himself, and take up his cross daily and follow Me. For whoever wishes to save his life will lose it, but whoever loses his life for My sake, he is the one who will save it. For what is a man profited if he gains the whole world, and loses or forfeits himself?'" To gain the world is immediate gratification, whereas to lose your soul is the verdict of the scales of spiritual justice. To take up your cross and follow Christ requires an eternal perspective.

What about the disciples? Did they live their best life now? Eleven of the twelve disciples met a martyr's fate, and the last died while exiled on the island of Patmos. Stephen was stoned in the book of Acts. History tells us Paul was beheaded and Peter was crucified upside down. The brother of Jesus was thrown from the temple and beaten to death. Living for Christ has often meant dying a martyr's death. The foundation of an eternal perspective will lead to an understanding that reduces the need for immediate gratification and encourages efforts that lay up rewards in heaven. This fundamental shift turns you from a consumer into a producer.

Quit Consuming and Start Producing

The shift from immediate gratification to an eternal perspective changes church on every level for the individual Christian. For example, you will no longer desire to be entertained as much as you will desire to learn more about the Word of God. You will no longer be as concerned about the slide in the children's play area as you will be about making sure your child is biblically literate. You will come to church to sing praises to your Lord and not to listen to your favorite style of music. And when the group onstage prevents you from singing, you will grow frustrated because you came to give and not just consume. You will no longer see the offering as the preacher's way of building his kingdom, but you will see the opportunity to give as a small token of gratitude for what you have been given. You will begin to pray that your own children may be missionaries in a developing country because all of sudden the gospel becomes more important than a three-car garage. You will not desire to be a member of a church where only cool people attend. Instead you will want to learn from your elders, care for the widows, be a father to the fatherless, minister to the orphans; and you will find fellowship among those who don't fall into your same economic or racial class.

Put another way, people will go to church not asking what the church can do for them, but what they can do for the church. Easy Christianity will soon become empty calories with negative long-term consequences. Most pastors already understand, and congregants need to be taught, that one day the spiritual scales of justice will weigh your decisions at the feet of Jesus Christ. The church staff will no longer be viewed as the hired gun to present the gospel. It is the job of each Christian to share the gospel. The church staff equips the body for works of service. You will grow tired of long illustrations that may be creative, cute, and entertaining, while you desire the depths and riches of God's Word to be expounded in a way that increases your love of Christ and glorifies God. The goal is to move from milk to meat where spiritual baby food will no longer appeal. This is the process of mature Christianity.

America must understand that its obsession with easy Christianity leads to severe spiritual judgment. My decision for fast food resulted in the negative consequence of increased physical weight. Your decision for easy Christianity will one day result in the negative consequence of spiritual unhealthiness and immaturity. Whether these consequences are demonstrated in the lack of your ability to answer the spiritual questions of a loved one, the lack of understanding at the moment of tragedy or at the judgment seat of Christ, make no mistake, Galatians 6:7 says, "Do not be deceived, God is not mocked; for whatever a man sows, this he will also reap."

Quitting McChurch—the Church's Decision in Eternal Perspective

McDonald's long-term effects on the health of consumers eventually led to lawsuits against the corporate giant. A class-action lawsuit filed by two teenagers claimed that McDonald's used false advertising and that McDonald's food contributed to health problems, including making them fat. These girls apparently thought the business had some long-term responsibility to its customers. However, the courts threw out the lawsuit, determining that McDonald's was not accountable for contributing to an unhealthy lifestyle.[5] After all, everyone knows that eating fast food will contribute to weight gain and is unhealthy. Americans continue to do it, but we know better. The U.S. House of Representatives even stepped in by passing a bill that banned obesity lawsuits against restaurant and food manufacturers.[6] Until now, consensus has been that the consumer cannot blame the business for poor choices even if the business contributes to obesity or unhealthiness.

While the legal court determined McDonald's was not legally accountable, the trial moved to the moral court of public opinion in 2004, when the movie *Super Size Me* hit the big screen.[7] In this documentary-style film, Morgan Spurlock decided to eat nothing but McDonald's for every meal for thirty days. Everyone knew the results would be bad for him, but few anticipated the rapid onset of health problems. Within the first week he gained ten pounds, and by the second week his doctors asked him to stop. While my own personal bad choices over a prolonged period led to negative results, this documentary demonstrated in a shorter time frame just how detrimental fast food is for the body.

In the discussion of quitting McChurch, we contend that McChurch does not provide a healthy situation for the spiritual growth of the consumer. Unlike McDonald's, McChurch will be tried in a moral court where faithfulness to God and His Word rule supreme. After all, Christ founded the church. Christ died for the church. Christ redeemed the church.

The Church Is Accountable

The Christians who make up the church or lead the church will one day give account for their actions. First Corinthians 3 discusses Christ as the foundation of the church, and Paul tells any man to "be careful how he builds on it." He also states in 1 Corinthians 3:13–15, "Each man's work will become evident; for the day will show it because it is to be revealed with fire; and the fire itself will test the quality of each man's work. If any man's work which he has built on it remains, he will receive a reward. If any man's work is burned up, he will suffer loss; but he himself will be saved, yet so as through fire."

In the book of Revelation, John records seven letters from Jesus to the various churches in which Christ issues judgment on the actions of those churches. To the church at Ephesus, John writes, "But I have this against you, that you have left your first love. Therefore remember from where you have fallen, and repent and do the deeds you did at first; or else I am coming to you and will remove your lampstand out of its place—unless you repent" (Rev. 2:4–5).

To the church in Pergamum, he writes, "But I have a few things against you, because you have there some who hold the teaching of Balaam, who kept teaching Balak to put a stumbling block before the sons of Israel, to eat things sacrificed to idols and to commit acts of immorality. So you also have some who in the same way hold the teaching of the Nicolaitans. Therefore repent; or else I am coming to you quickly, and I will make war against them with the sword of My mouth" (Rev. 2:14–16).

He also writes portions against the churches at Thyatira and Sardis. Perhaps most applicable to us today, John writes to the church at Laodicea in Revelation 3:15–19,

> I know your deeds, that you are neither cold nor hot; I wish that you were cold or hot. So because you are lukewarm, and neither hot nor cold, I will spit you out of My mouth. Because you say, "I am rich, and have become wealthy, and have need of nothing," and you do not know that you are wretched and miserable and poor and blind and naked, I advise you to buy from Me gold refined by fire so that you may become rich, and white garments so that you may clothe yourself, and that the shame of your nakedness will not be revealed; and eye salve to anoint your eyes so that you may see. Those whom I love, I reprove and discipline; therefore be zealous and repent.

God will judge the actions of the churches, and those churches that have contributed to McChurching will not fare well.

Providing for the Need and Not the Want

The Bible is clear that humans have a sin problem and that the grace of Jesus Christ is all that can solve that problem. The Bible also tells us that the heart of man is "more deceitful than all else and is desperately sick; who can understand it?" (Jer. 17:9). The Bible also tells us in 2 Timothy of a time to come when people will not endure sound doctrine. Paul writes concerning this in 2 Timothy 4:1–5:

> I solemnly charge you in the presence of God and
> of Christ Jesus, who is to judge the living and the
> dead, and by His appearing and His kingdom:
> preach the word; be ready in season and out
> of season; reprove, rebuke, exhort, with great
> patience and instruction. For the time will come
> when they will not endure sound doctrine; but
> wanting to have their ears tickled, they will accu-
> mulate for themselves teachers in accordance
> to their own desires, and will turn away their ears
> from the truth and will turn aside to myths. But
> you, be sober in all things, endure hardship,
> do the work of an evangelist, fulfill your ministry.

The time has truly come when the spiritual consumers have
"accumulate[d] for themselves teachers in accordance to their own
desires." This result is inevitable. The wickedness of man will always
allow him to drift to those things that make him feel good and not
to the prophet who calls for his sin and demands repentance. The
problem arises when, because of power, influence, and the size of the
ministry, some who merely tickle ears have become the example to
be imitated. Paul says these ministries "turn away their ears from the
truth." Paul contrasts these ministries with what Timothy should do,
by stating, "But you …"

The obligation of one Christian to another is not immediately
gratifying but produces long-term health. This principle can be
clearly seen in Philippians 2:3–4: "Do nothing from selfishness or

empty conceit, but with humility of mind regard one another as more important than yourselves; do not merely look out for your own personal interests, but also for the interests of others." The attitude of looking out for others' interests more than our own would indicate that the long-term spiritual health of a person comes first.

Additionally, church discipline requires this consideration. We confront not because it is fun or easy but because the long-term health of the sinner needs to be addressed. This motivation also provides the impetus for evangelism. Evangelism recognizes that eternal destinies will be determined by immediate decisions and that the confrontation with the sinner over spiritual lostness addresses eternal destinies. Confrontationally sharing the gospel may appear harsh, or closed minded, but the motivation for sharing the gospel is the eternal destiny and well-being of the person and ultimately brings glory to Jesus Christ.

When the size and the sphere of influence of the congregation measure success more than faithfulness to the Word and the spreading of the gospel, then McChurch has taken hold. The consumer replaces God's Word as the foundation for the ministry. The desires of the masses differ from the demands of Christ. *In order to quit McChurch, the church must decide that its duty and obligation is to provide for the true spiritual needs of the people and not the desires of the consumer.* After all, the church worships an audience of One—Jesus Christ—and is accountable only to Him.[8]

An attitude that builds a church at the sacrifice of long-term spiritual health or a church that takes shortcuts to immediate success has ignored the eternal perspective. Such a church has failed to consider the interests of others before its own. For this reason, we must quit McChurch by providing for the need and not for the want.

The Power of the Church Comes from Christ
The apostle Paul wrote in 1 Corinthians 2:1–5,

> And when I came to you, brethren, I did not come with superiority of speech or of wisdom, proclaiming to you the testimony of God. For I determined to know nothing among you except Jesus Christ, and Him crucified. I was with you in weakness and in fear and in much trembling, and my message and my preaching were not in persuasive words of wisdom, but in demonstration of the Spirit and of power, so that your faith would not rest on the wisdom of men, but on the power of God.

If we are to quit McChurch, we must recognize that it is not our creativity, not our entertainment, and not our performance that bring about real-life change. The American church has lost its understanding of the power of prayer. The prayer meeting has become nonexistent. The American church has lost its understanding of the power of the Spirit. Even human wisdom and marketing methods can manufacture success. While marketing techniques can put bodies in the seats, no one knows what is truly happening in the spiritual depths of the soul.

As previously noted in this work, much of the growth in new churches comes from transfer growth and not pagan conversions.

The American church has also lost its understanding of the power of God's Word. It is God's Word that will not return void. It is the gospel that is the power of God unto salvation. When we rely solely on creative videos and creative words to persuade people, then the question must be asked, "Who are we leading people to?" You should ask yourself if McChurch leads masses to follow the wisdom of a man or the success of a method rather than introducing them to the simplicity of the Master. Again, we are not advocating boring, dull preaching, but McChurch has placed the proverbial cart before the horse. The creativity becomes the message and the gospel becomes minimized. When the listener remembers the illustration more than the message, we have lost our meaning. When the preacher spends more time on the delivery than on researching the depths of Scripture, then whose messenger are we? The very nature of McChurch stands in direct contrast to the words of Paul in 1 Corinthians.

Conclusion

This summer I (Thomas) went to Disney World during the same time I wrote much of my part of the content for this work. I looked all around Disney for different aspects of entertainment and consumerism. Like the July heat, I found these aspects everywhere; however, the most improbable illustration came from my thirteen-year-old nephew. The group that accompanied me on the Disney trip included five kids ranging in age from an almost two-year-old, a two-and-a-half-year-old, a three-year-old, a ten-year-old, to a thirteen-year-old. As you can imagine, planning a trip that would meet the personal desires of each of these kids would require a split in the group, but all of the adults wanted to experience Disney as a group. Suddenly, my thirteen-year-old nephew said, "I want to see the little kids, [including his cousin]. I don't mind going on the little-kid rides."

With these few words, I felt a sense of pride in my nephew, and many of our problems disappeared. Both my nephew and my niece spent the entire day going from "fun ride" to "kiddie ride" without ever complaining. The group dynamic developed in such a way that selfish individualism was not present. In fact, the entire group endured certain things that did not meet individual desires. For example, my niece sat through a show about the American presidents. I, on the other hand, sat idly by as the women went shopping. At the end of the day, everyone felt good about the trip. Everyone had certain important aspects maintained, but no one left feeling slighted because we all put the needs of the group before individual desires.

We wish that our churches would put the needs of the group before individual desires. This too would solve many problems. In individual churches, this mentality would help solve the worship wars. The younger generation could learn to appreciate the great hymns that the older generation listened to at their conversion, or baptism, or other special moments. The older generation could experience some of the louder and more contemporary music that frames the hallmarks of the younger generation's spiritual journey.

This mentality would also help our churches. Rather than competing with other churches of like belief, we should cooperate with those churches. The days of the community thanksgiving services have for better or worse ended; however, we can cooperate on evangelistic efforts together for the sake of the bigger group—God's kingdom. Such emphasis also recognizes that not every new believer needs to be a member of your church. As long as they receive proper teaching, we can and sometimes should encourage our faithful members to help plant new churches, revive old, dying churches, or help out sister churches. Our individualistic society has led to individualistic churches. While we may cooperate for overseas missions, we seldom cooperate for evangelism right around the corner. Perhaps such cooperation fulfills what it means to be missional. The missional mind-set allows churches to recognize fulfillment in reaching God's mission.

This summer, my thirteen-year-old nephew reinforced a lesson to me when he said it was okay to ride "It's a Small World After All." I hope our churches realize that "It's a Small World After All" and that it all belongs to the one true God.

DRIVE THRU ⬆

I'll Take That to Go

- ▫ Living for the now encourages immediate gratification, whereas the Bible presents an eternal perspective of living for eternity.

- ▫ We must make a personal decision to stop viewing church as the provider of a spiritual product.

- ▫ Ask not what can the church do for you, but ask what can you do for the church.

- ▫ We should come as Paul did with the simplicity of the gospel, demonstrating the power of God rather than the wisdom of people.

Health Inspector

- ▫ How does your church prepare others to suffer injustice, tribulation, and even persecution for the cause of Christ?

- ▫ If God brought revival through another church rather than yours, what would your reaction be?

- ▫ According to 1 Corinthians 3, how will your works fare at the judgment?

- ▫ What causes people to come to church? What role do creativity and cultural sensitivity play?

- ▫ Why not plant a church? Oh, sorry, I think we've asked that one already.

Notes

Growing Waistlines in the Church Buffet Life

1. For more information about McDonald's history, visit http://www.McDonalds.com/corp/about/mcd_history_pg1.html (accessed Sept. 10, 2008). Even more interesting is a quick visit to the original McDonald's store in Des Plaines, a suburb of Chicago. While you can't get burgers and fries there, you can visit the McDonald's museum and see the famous Multimixers that started the whole thing.

2. "Twenty Years of the Big Mac Index," *Economist,* May 25, 2006.

3. George Ritzer, *McDonaldization: The Reader* (Thousand Oaks, CA: Pine Forge Press, 2002), 7.

Chapter 1: Over One Billion Served: Effective vs. Efficient Churches

1. John Yeats, "Jena Revival to Enter 7th Week," *Baptist Press,* March 27, 2008, http://www.bpnews.net/bpnews.asp?id=27713 (accessed Sept. 10, 2008).

2. T. D. Allman, "The Theme-Parking, Megachurching, Franchising, Exurbing, McMansioning of America: How Walt Disney Changed Everything," in *National Geographic,* vol. 211 no. 3 (March 2007), 103.

3. Derrick Jensen as interviewed by George Ritzer, *McDonaldization: The Reader,* 29.

4. http://www.driveinchurch.net/ (accessed Sept. 10, 2008).

5. "At the Drive-in Church Photo Essay," *Time,* http://www.time.

com/time/photoessays/2006/drive_in_church/ (accessed Sept. 10, 2008).

6. Deirdre Cox Baker, "Church Hosts 'Drive-Thru' Sunday Services," *Quad City Times*, May 26, 2005, http://www.qctimes. com/articles/2005/05/26/local/export93493.txt (accessed Sept. 10, 2008).

7. Ibid.

8. http://mccqc.com/index.html.

9. "Evangelical Church Operates Drive-through Prayer Booth," http://www.gamma.fnphoto.com/stories/2229/index.htm (accessed Sept. 11, 2008).

10. "'Need Prayer' Church Offers Drive-Through 'Prayer Booth,'" *Baptist Press,* http://www.sbcbaptistpress.org/bpnews. asp?ID=16798 (accessed Sept. 11, 2008); or "... Dear God, Please Supersize That, Amen," http://www.thefreelibrary.com/. ..+And%2c+dear+God%2c+please+supersize+that%2c+amen-a0106914966 (accessed Sept. 11, 2008). For a photo tour see http://www.gamma.fnphoto.com/stories/2229/index.htm.

11. http://www.30minuteworship.com/.

Chapter 2: Do I Get Fries with That?: Predictability in the Pew

1. Daniel Gross, "The Shrinking Gap: The Ultimate '90s Brand Slides toward the Murky Middle," *Slate,* http://www.slate.com/ id/2137742 (accessed Oct. 13, 2006).

Chapter 3: Supersized for the Kingdom: Counting the Numbers

1. Allman, in *National Geographic*, 102.

2. For more information on George Mueller's life, see Arthur T.

Pierson, *George Müller of Bristol and His Witness to a Prayer-Hearing God* (Grand Rapids, MI: Kregel, 1999).

3. James B. Twitchell, *Shopping for God: How Christianity Went from in Your Heart to in Your Face* (New York: Simon and Schuster, 2007), 61–62.

4. Twitchell, *Shopping for God*, 3. Twitchell argues that megachurches "are run by a very market-savvy class of speculators whom I will call pastorpreneurs." "Visioneering" is the term Disney cast members and staff use for dream sessions about the future of their corporation.

5. Veli-Matti Karkkainen, *An Introduction to Ecclesiology: Ecumenical, Historical and Global Perspectives* (Downers Grove, IL: InterVarsity, 2002), 214.

Chapter 4: Have It My Way: Control and the Church

1. Dan Kimball, *They Like Jesus but Not the Church: Insights from Emerging Congregations* (Grand Rapids, MI: Zondervan, 2007).

2. George Barna and Frank Viola, *Pagan Christianity? Exploring the Roots of Our Church Practices* (Ventura, CA: Barna Books, 2008), xx.

3. P. D. Holley and D. E. Wright Jr., "A Sociology of Rib Joints," in *McDonaldization Revisited: Critical Essays on Consumer Culture*, Mark Alfino et al., eds. (Westport, CT: Praeger Paperbacks, 1998), 73–82.

4. Leonard Sweet has an interesting take on this idea in his *The Gospel according to Starbucks* (Colorado Springs: WaterBrook Press, 2007).

5. John Drane, *The McDonaldization of the Church* (London: Darton, Longman, and Todd, Ltd., 2000), 54.

6. Based on Ritzer, *McDonaldization of Society*. The four areas discussed are based upon the categories he developed in his book.

Chapter 5: Chicken McWhat?: The By-Products of McChurch

1. For those not familiar with Baptist church polity, I would encourage you to see Mark Dever, *A Display of God's Glory* (Washington DC: 9Marks, 2001).

2. www.9marks.com.

3. For more information see www.secondlife.com or www.lifechurch.tv.

4. Karkkainen, *An Introduction to Ecclesiology*, 228.

Chapter 6: Another Milkshake, but Where's the Beef?: Sugar or Sustenance in the Teaching of the Church?

1. Our thanks to Allison Sindelir for tracking down the true story of the McShake from McDonald's Corporate.

2. "Don't Be Original, Be Effective!" *Pastors.com Ministry Toolbox,* http://www.pastors.com/RWMT/article.asp?ArtID=9230 (accessed March 15, 2008). See Sjogren's response to critics from the world of academia at http://www.jumpstartchurch.com/2007/06/10/becoming-a-better-communicator-is-easier-than-you-think-pt-1/ (accessed Sept. 22, 2008).

3. L. R. Scarborough, *My Conception of the Gospel Ministry* (Nashville: Sunday School Board, 1935), 72.

4. "Don't Be Original, Be Effective!" http://www.pastors.com/RWMT/article.asp?ArtID=9230; see a response to this article

by Ray Van Neste, "FIRST-PERSON: Pastoral Plagiarism," Baptist Press, Sept. 15, 2006, http://www.bpnews.net/bpnews. asp?ID=23988 (accessed Sept. 11, 2008).

5. Suzanne Sataline, "That Sermon You Heard on Sunday May Be from the Web," *Wall Street Journal Online*, Nov. 15, 2006, http:// online.wsj.com/articleSB116355983749723495-lMyQjAxM-DE2NjEzNTUxNTU5Wj.html (accessed Sept. 11, 2008).

6. Scarborough, 69.

7. Ibid., 70–71.

8. Ibid., 72–73.

9. Elesha Coffman, "Mega-Ministers," *Christianity Today,* http:// www.christianitytoday.com/chnews/2001/jun15.html (accessed Oct. 9, 2008).

10. "Don't Be Original, Be Effective!" http://www.pastors.com/ RWMT/article.asp?ArtID=9230.

11. "8 Principles for Preaching Others' Sermons," Sept. 3, 2006, http://www.twoorthree.net/2006/09/8_principles_fo.html (accessed Sept. 11, 2008).

12. "Don't Be Original, Be Effective!" http://www.pastors.com/ RWMT/article.asp?ArtID=9230.

13. "That Sermon You Heard on Sunday May Be from the Web," http://online.wsj.com/article/SB116355983749723495-lMyQ-jAxMDE2NjEzNTUxNTU5Wj.html.

14. April 30, 2005, *World Magazine* (20:17, 30–31). See http://www. narnia3.com/mt/Blog/Archives/000072.html.

15. Michael Luo, "A Pastor Who Plagiarized Finds a Congregation Willing to Forgive," *New York Times*, July 28, 2006, http://www. nytimes.com/2006/07/28/nyregion/28pastor.html?ex=1311739

200&en=e51e0153bcad49b1&ei=5088&partner=rssnyt&emc=
rss (accessed Sept. 11, 2008).

16. "That Sermon You Heard on Sunday May Be from the Web,"
http://online.wsj.com/article/SB116355983749723495-lMyQ-
jAxMDE2NjEzNTUxNTU5Wj.html.

17. Sarah Horn, "Plagiarism in the Pulpit," *Willow Magazine,*
issue 3, 2006, http://www.willowcreek.com/wcanews/story.
asp?id=WN02I32006 (accessed Sept. 11, 2008).

18. "The Problem with Borrowing Sermons," *Preaching Now,* vol.
4, no. 26, Aug. 2, 2005, http://www.preaching.com/newsletter/
preachingnow/archive_2005/08_02.htm (accessed Sept. 11,
2008). The article was first written here: http://www.sbts.edu/
resources/publications/sbjt/1999/1999Summer8.pdf.

19. David Cho, "Channeling God at the Video Café," *Washington
Post,* Sept. 5, 2004, http://www.washingtonpost.com/wp-dyn/
articles/A61998-2004Sep4.html (accessed Sept. 11, 2008);
for a reaction to this, read "Video Killed the Preacher Man,"
posted at Church Marketing Sucks, Sept. 9, 2004, http://www.
churchmarketingsucks.com/archives/2004/09/video_killed_
th.html (accessed Sept. 11, 2008).

20. Horn, "Plagiarism in the Pulpit."

21. "The Problem with Borrowing Sermons," http://www.preaching.
com/newsletter/preachingnow/archive_2005/08_02.htm.

22. Luo, "A Pastor Who Plagiarized...."

23. Ibid.

24. John MacArthur, "Fifteen Evil Consequences of Plexiglas Preaching," Pulpit—Shepherds' Fellowship, 2003, http://www.biblebb.
com/files/MAC/plexiglas-sf1.htm (accessed Sept. 11, 2008).

25.A personal testimony of this type of transformation can be read at http://www.9marks.org/partner/Article_Display_Page/0,,PTI D314526|CHID598014|CIID2190948,00.html (accessed Jan. 14, 2007).

Chapter 7: Happy Meals for All?: Theotainment in the Church

1. Jenny Deam, "Happy Meal Reaches Milestone," *Denver Post*, July 15, 2004, http://www.azcentral.com/ent/pop/ articles/0715happymeal15.html (accessed Sept. 11, 2008); the Happy Meal even has its own Web site now. See http://www. happymeal.com/en_US/#Home.

2. Ibid.

3. Ibid.

4. Neil Postman, *Amusing Ourselves to Death: Public Discourse in the Age of Show Business* (New York: Penguin, 2005).

5. Ibid., 76. Ironically, Postman stated this prior to the mainstream-ing of the Internet and the popularity of alternative-reality games such as Second Life.

6. Nathan Hatch, *The Democratization of American Christianity* (New Haven: Yale University Press, 1989).

7. Twitchell, *Shopping for God*, 3.

8. Ibid., 153–154.

9. Ibid., 70.

10.Ibid., 273. For additional information on the consumer mentality and religion, see Vincent J. Miller, *Consuming Religion: Christian Faith and Practice in a Consumer Culture* (New York: Continuum, 2005); and John Kavanaugh, *Following Christ in a Consumer Soci-ety* (New York: Orbis Books, 2006).

11.Ibid., 24.

12.Greg Hawkins and Cally Parkinson, *Reveal: Where Are You?* (South Barrington, IL: Willow Creek Association, 2007).

13.Postman, *Amusing Ourselves to Death,* 121.

14.Skye Jethani, "All We Like Sheep: Is Our Insistence on Choices Leading Us Astray?" *Leadership Journal* 27:3 (Summer 2006), 30.

15.Ibid., 30.

16.Phil Lewis, "Mixed Reactions to Closed-Circuit Preaching," *Christian Post*, Nov. 29, 2004, http://www.christianpost.com/ article/20041129/19073_Mixed_Reactions_to_Closed-Circuit_ Preaching.htm (accessed Sept. 11, 2008).

17.Ibid.

18.Ibid.

19.Barna, *Revolution.*

20.Ibid., 31.

21.Ibid., 31.

22.Cho, "Channeling God at the Video Café," http://www.washing-tonpost.com/wp-dyn/articles/A61998-2004Sep4.html.

23.Ken Dean, "Video Venues to the Rescue," *Church Executive Magazine,* vol. 2003, issue 10, http://www.churchexecutive.com/ article.asp?IndexID=237 (accessed Sept. 11, 2008).

24.Ibid.

25.Ibid.

26.Ibid.

27.Jethani, "All We Like Sheep," 31.

28.Dean, "Video Venues to the Rescue," http://www.churchexecu-tive.com/article.asp?IndexID=237.

Chapter 8: The Multisite Movement: Feeding Consumerism

1. Calvin Pearson, "Sheep, Serpents & Doves," *Preaching*, vol. 24, no 1 (July/Aug 2008): 16.

2. In addition to planting churches and pastoring, Gene Getz also served as a professor at Dallas Theological Seminary, is a noted author and speaker, and currently leads a ministry called the Center for Church Renewal. All information is taken from an interview on 10 July 2008.

3. William Chadwick, *Stealing Sheep: The Church's Hidden Problems with Transfer Growth* (Downers Grove, IL: InterVarsity, 2001), 64. See especially chapter 4, "Counting Sheep" and chapter 5, "Fleecing the Flock."

4. Ibid.

5. http://www.lifechurch.tv/.

Chapter 9: Expanding the Franchise: Extending Your Brand or the Kingdom's?

1. Geoff Surratt, Greg Ligon, and Warren Bird, *The Multi-Site Church Revolution* (Grand Rapids, MI: Zondervan, 2006), 53.

2. Bruce Horovitz, "Fast-Food Giants Try Value Menus," *USA Today*, http://www.usatoday.com/money/industries/food/2002-09-11-burger-king-99cents_x.htm (accessed Sept. 11, 2008).

3. "Is the Multi-Campus Church Concept Biblical?" JDGreear.com, Nov. 23, 2007, http://jdgreear.typepad.com/my_weblog/2007/11/is-the-multi-ca.html (accessed Sept. 11, 2008).

4. Ibid.

5. Eilat Mazar, *The Complete Guide to the Temple Mount Excavations* (Jerusalem: Shalom Academic Research, 2002), 27.

6. http://football.ballparks.com/NFL/CarolinaPanthers/index.htm.

7. Surratt, Ligon, and Bird, *The Multi-Site Church Revolution*, 92.

8. Ibid., 140.

9. Ibid., 91.

10. Ibid.

11. http://united.lifechurch.tv/.

12. http://www.creativepastors.com/merge.php.

13. Interview with Gene Getz, 10 July 2008.

Chapter 10: The Coming of McDenominations: How Multisite Strategies May Bring the End of Church Autonomy

1. Surratt, Ligon, and Bird, *The Multi-Site Church Revolution*, 9.

2. Ross King, "Happy," from *Welcome to America,* www.RossKing-Music.com. Used by permission.

3. Surratt, Ligon, and Bird, *The Multi-Site Church Revolution*, 10.

4. John Piper, "Treasuring Christ Together as a Church on Multiple Campuses," *Desiring God,* Nov. 4, 2007, http://www.desiringgod.org/ResourceLibrary/Sermons/ByDate/2007/2479_Treasuring_Christ_Together_as_a_Church_on_Multiple_Campuses/ (accessed Nov. 5, 2007).

5. Information on LifeChurch.tv can be obtained from the Web site www.lifechurch.tv, and the Internet campus can be found at http://www.lifechurch.tv/?p=752 (accessed Nov. 5, 2007).

6. Second Life is a virtual world that features businesses, educational opportunities, churches, and many other items where real dollars exchange hands for services and the purchase of virtual space. For more information, one may consult Andrea Foster, "Professor Avatar," *Chronicle of Higher Education* (Sept. 21, 2007) http://

chronicle.com/subscribe/login?url=/weekly/v54/i04/04a02401. htm; Michael J. Bugeja, "Second Thoughts about Second Life" *The Chronicle of Higher Education* (Sept. 14, 2007) http:// chronicle.com/subscribe/login?url=/weekly/v54/i03/03c00101. htm; Andrea Foster, "The Avatars of Research," *The Chronicle of Higher Education* (Sept. 30, 2005), http://chronicle.com/weekly/ v52/i06/06a03501.htm; and Andrea Foster, "Harvard to Offer Law Course in 'Virtual World,'" *Chronicle of Higher Education* (Sept. 8, 2006), http://chronicle.com/weekly/v53/i03/03a02902. htm; "Reuters Opens Virtual News Bureau," http://www.msnbc. msn.com/id/15289096/wid/11915829/GT1/8618/ (accessed Nov. 3, 2007); "If Second Life Isn't a Game What Is It?" http:// www.msnbc.msn.com/id/17538999/ (accessed Nov. 3, 2007); and "Second Life, IBM Opens Virtual World Borders," http:// www.msnbc.msn.com/id/21218506/ (accessed Nov. 3, 2007). To access the virtual world, go to www.secondlife.com (accessed Nov. 5, 2007).

7. NBC Nightly News interview, "Give Me That Online Religion," Don Teague, May 21, 2007. The video can be seen here: http://video.msn. com/?mkt=en-us&brand=msnbc&fg=email&vid=003d2240-7893-4d6e-b5b6-735dd9ce5f07&from=00. Transcript at http:// www.msnbc.msn.com/id/18789168/from/ET/ (accessed Nov. 5 2007).

8. This was encouraged in one of the announcements mentioned on their Web site when the Sunday service would be partaking of Communion. The information appears only periodically as Communion occurs, and no citation can be provided.

9. Surratt, Ligon, and Bird, *The Multi-Site Church Revolution*, 17.

10. Ibid., 11–12.

11. Ibid., 18.

12. From   http://www.merriamwebster.com/dictionary/denomination (accessed Jan. 11, 2007).

13. Surratt, Ligon, and Bird, *The Multi-Site Church Revolution*, 205–08, notes Community Presbyterian Church, First United Methodist Church, Gulf Breeze United Methodist Church, Immanuel United Methodist, Redeemer Presbyterian, St. Luke's United Methodist Church, and Stillwater United Methodist Church. The vast majority of the churches would fall in the Free church movement.

14. Wayne Grudem, *Systematic Theology: An Introduction to Biblical Doctrine* (Grand Rapids, MI: Zondervan, 1995), 923–36, contains a good discussion of the various forms of structure.

15. Although I have stated that they must work through the system, any denominational structure that has the top of the organization owning the property even in a multisite structure leaves the local congregation with very little opportunity for action other than going to court. For example, in order for an Episcopal church to withdraw, it had to reach an agreement to sell the property and was allowed to use the facilities it built for only a few months before needing to relocate. See the following for some of the discussion: http://www.livingchurch.org/news/news-updates/2006/04/21/bishops-give-notice-on-property;   http://www.livingchurch.org/news/news-updates/2003/11/03/property-ownership-at-heart-of-lawsuit-in-pittsburgh ;   and http://www.livingchurch.org/news/news-updates/2004/12/27/california-high-court-rules-parishes-may-keep-property.

16. See Pat McCaughan, "From Columbus: Episcopal Church Elects First Woman Presiding Bishop," *Episcopal News Service,* June 18, 2006, http://www.episcopalchurch.org/3577_76174_ENG_HTM.htm (accessed Jan. 13, 2007). For more information on the controversy surrounding Gene Robinson, see "Mixed Feelings as First Openly Gay Anglican Bishop Is Consecrated," *Episcopal News Service,* Nov. 4, 2003, http://www.episcopalchurch.org/3577_21445_ENG_HTM.htm (accessed Jan. 13, 2007).

17. Information about this association can be found at http://www.willowcreek.com/.

18. Other resources for joining can be found at https://www.willowcreek.com/membership/member_benefits.asp.

19. In fairness, most multisite proponents do not like this terminology; however, for clear discussion, it is necessary to give some label to the original congregation. See Surratt, Ligon, and Bird, *The Multi-Site Church Revolution*, 90: "Almost every multisite church decides not to refer to the original location as the main campus or the mother church or even the mother ship. This terminology can easily communicate to the venues and sites birthed from the original campus that they are second-class."

20. Surratt, Ligon, and Bird, *The Multi-Site Church Revolution,* 7.

21. Ibid., 33.

22. John Calvin, *Institutes of the Christian Religion,* in *Library of Christian Classics,* trans. by F. L. Battles, ed. John T. McNeill (Louisville: Westminster, 1960), 1066. He stated that Acts 14:23 demonstrated congregational affirmation "by a show of hands in every church." This is his interpretation of χειροτονέω. In addition, he noted that Cyprian implied congregational

affirmation by insisting that the choosing of the bishop be done in the presence of the people.

Chapter 11: Quitting McChurch

1. http://www.McDonald's.com/app_controller.nutrition.index1. html.

2. http://www.subway.com/applications/NutritionInfo/nutrition-list.aspx?CountryCode=USA&ID=sandwich.

3. http://www.mayoclinic.com/health/exercise/SM00109.

4. Ibid.

5. "McDonald's Obesity Suit Thrown Out," CNN, Sept. 4, 2003, http://www.cnn.com/2003/LAW/09/04/McDonald's.suit/ index.html (accessed Sept. 11, 2008); Jonathan Wald, "Lawyers Revise Obesity Lawsuit against McDonald's," CNN, Feb. 21, 2003, http://www.cnn.com/2003/LAW/02/21/obesity.lawsuit/ (accessed Sept. 11, 2008); and "Fat Suit vs. McDonald's Rein-stated," CBS News, Jan. 25, 2005, http://www.cbsnews.com/ stories/2005/01/25/national/main669369.shtml (accessed Sept. 11, 2008).

6. Todd Zwillich, "House Votes to Ban 'Cheeseburger' Law-suits," WebMD Health News, http://www.webmd.com/diet/ news/20051019/house-votes-to-ban-cheeseburger-lawsuits (accessed Sept. 11, 2008).

7. http://www.imdb.com/title/tt0390521/.

8. For pastors seeking positive help in the theology or practice of the church, we would encourage them to visit www.baptisttheology. org or www.9marks.org. While we may not agree with everything on these sites, they are committed to helping the local church.